# Journey to Mega

# Journey to Mega

## From Psychic to Mystic

### By

### Veronica Vader

1stBooks – rev. 12/20/00

# Index

v

# PREFACE

My purpose in writing this book is not to instruct but to share. Perhaps something in this book will seem familiar or help to clear up some confusion.

Some of the events in this book may be difficult to accept because they seem so far-fetched. I ask that the reader keep an open mind and remember that "all things are possible with God."

I myself found some of the things that happened difficult to accept but they were usually explained so that they made sense.

I have learned that there are really no limits and nothing is "written in stone."

Looking back, I realize my experiences are quite wide. I include some episodes from each area.

These are my personal experiences in clairaudience, clairvoyance, healing, thought-forms, discarnates and experiences on this level and on the inner planes. They include UFOs, walk-ins and reincarnation.

I am sharing some communications from my higher self. These contain information given to me about angels and "evil beings" and many other subjects.

Also, I write about actual happenings on the physical level and other assorted topics.

I do not profess to be an expert in any of the above areas, as I am still learning. Every answer brings new questions.

Hopefully, my readers will find this book interesting as well as informative. I found it enjoyable to write much to my surprise.

The various experiences I write about are in proper sequence for the most part. They are not necessarily the experience of one "personality", as will be explained in the chapter on "Walk-ins".

I do not intend for this book to be a "text" book. Rather, I prefer to think of it as a conversation between like-minded people.

# INTRODUCTION

People have often asked when I became aware that I was psychic. Actually, it didn't occur to me until quite late in life. Thinking back, I recall a few things that may have indicated that I was psychic as a child. At the time, I didn't realize that I might have had any special gift in this area.

There are memories of going to the neighborhood "Mom and Pop" grocery store where they had a candy counter. One of the things they had to attract children to spend their pennies was a little game. They had small wrapped caramels, tubular in shape, for one cent. If you picked one that had a white center, you won a large caramel sucker. I won so many suckers that the owner asked me how I knew which ones to choose! Since they were wrapped, we were allowed to handle them. The lucky ones "felt" different to me. After that, I was not allowed to handle the little candies, but I still won more often than not. I still "felt" the white centers just by looking at them.

I could also see energy fields around trees and plants. Later, I learned I was seeing auras and could see them around people as well.

On one occasion, when I was in the third or fourth grade, we had a Halloween party in our classroom. One of the contests was to see who could draw the best jack-o-lantern face without being able to see the blackboard. We had to stand with our backs to the board and draw it over our heads. I won, because I could "see" what I was drawing.

Also, my mother claimed that whenever she had a really bad headache she would ask me to rub her forehead and the pain would go away. Apparently, I had some healing ability at an early age, but I didn't think anything about it. I thought it was the rubbing, the physical contact alone, which caused her headache to go away. I still feel that this was a part of the healing process. Another thing I remember is that if I really wanted something, I would get it without even mentioning it to anyone. Somehow, someone would give me whatever it was that I was thinking strongly about.

Again, I want to say that I do not consider myself to be an authority on any of the matters discussed in this book. I am only sharing some of my experiences which some may find interesting and perhaps helpful in understanding their own experiences. I fully understand that all the wonderful events I speak of are not due to any special powers that I have, but to the power of God, who dwells in all of us.

Some of the experiences I relate happened on the "inner planes", and some of the things that were told to me there may be very difficult for some to understand and accept, not to say find controversial. I can only tell of these events as I experienced them. They are "my" truth, and I do not ask that anyone accept them as their truth but read with an open mind.

I wrote this book after many people had told me through the years that I ought to write one. I had no intention of doing so because, at this time of my life, I just wanted to enjoy life-to take it easy. Besides, I had no idea of how to even begin to write a book. I've always been an avid reader, but the idea of writing a book seemed an insurmountable challenge. But, people kept insisting that I do it. So, I halfheartedly started going through some old notebooks in which I had jotted down information about some things that had occurred. I had done this only for my own records. Additionally, I came across many letters from people who had asked for help not only for themselves, but others, and had received it.

Gradually, I have come to feel that I was supposed to write this book primarily to help others "on the path". I want to aid them in their understanding of some of the things that may have happened to them so that they would know they weren't alone "out there". Perhaps it will help others to realize how much more there is than what they've always accepted as "the way things are".

As I started writing, I remembered more and more. Although some of these things happened over twenty years ago, they are as fresh in my mind as though they had just happened yesterday. Some of the things about which I write may not be placed in the exact order in which they occurred since I have tried to group related experiences together. However, they are all written exactly as they happened. The circumstances or the information have not been changed.

I must say here that all of the beings I have met and communicated with on the "inner planes" or in an altered state of consciousness are as real to me and as dear to me as my earthly family and friends. The places to where I've been taken and in which I do my "work" are as real to me as my own home and places I go to here on this plane.

Though some of the things I've experienced may at first seem too incredible and fantastic to comprehend, I find I actually have references to them here on earth. For instance, I was once taken to a field of incredibly beautiful flowers of every possible color. As a gentle breeze blew through them, each color produced a musical note, filling the air with music such as one may never hear on earth. Conversely, the musical notes produced gorgeous colors as they soared above the flowers, changing and blending endlessly. At this time, I saw "draperies" such as those produced by the Northern Lights that also produced music as they rippled and flowed. Many years later, I saw the Disney animated production Fantasia that had scenes, which recalled all of this to my mind. Had the creator of this fantasy for Disney been where I had been? I believe all creative people are in an altered state of consciousness as they do their work.

All the experiences I've had on the "inner planes" removed any fear of death that I may have had. In fact, I'm looking forward to it with joyful anticipation, since I've had a glimpse of the peace, joy, beauty and marvelous loving, caring beings that await us there. Not that I believe I've experienced all that is there, having only had a toe in the door, so to speak. But I do know it will be a place of continued learning and growth.

I have found that the more I learn, the more I realize how little I know, and am filled with questions always.

Although all my life I have been very interested in things that were unusual, it wasn't until my late forties that I began to develop an insatiable interest in metaphysical things. I searched for and literally devoured any and all books on these subjects, even reading during meals and any other times I could manage. Since I still had young children, it wasn't easy. My husband said I was in danger of becoming "unbalanced". I replied that, on the contrary, I was coming into balance. I felt that this was a very important part of my nature that had been neglected being wife, mother, homemaker, etc., and all the activity that went with trying to do a good job of all these things. So, I went on reading, studying, practicing all I could. I read hundreds of books, studied every kind of system I could find to enable me to function as I knew I could if I could just find the "key" to the inner planes.

During this time, I found that I could use healing energy to help others. However, there were so many other areas in which I wanted to become adept and I believed that I would be able to perform in many of these areas.

Faithfully practicing all the techniques, at last I could function as I thought I ought to be able to. I became a "practitioner", instead of a "petitioner". I was finally using my mind as God intended me to use it, as He intended all of us to do. I was not just asking God to do things for others and me. I was actually directing the power so generously given to all of us to bring about the desired results.

The most important thing I learned was that in order to get to a level of mind conducive to functioning as I wished, it was necessary to achieve a relaxed state of mind. I had to eliminate everything from my mind but that particular person or thing I wanted to work with. In other words, I had to reach a meditative state of mind. This is so important that I have devoted an entire chapter to it.

Trying some of the standard methods of meditation, but finding them too boring for me, I discovered that it was possible (and necessary) to reach a meditative state by relaxing completely. I learned to do this no matter what the circumstances might be or where I was at the time. It was important to me to depend on nothing but my own mind. I didn't want to feel that I needed incense, rituals, or certain objects. Dependence on these things would limit me as to where or when I could effectively use what I had learned.

At first, my primary interest was seeing what I could do with this newfound and enjoyable technique. Of course, healing was most important to me at that time and, I must say, results were achieved which I found most satisfying.

I always ask to see the cause of a condition or problem rather than working with symptoms. Symptoms can often be misleading. When I am given the cause, I then work psychically to correct the problem, doing whatever comes to me to do, often with the assistance of "other world" helpers. I then visualize the desired results. This method works on any sort of problem, but since I always work with "Divine Plan"; all results are not always as expected. It is important to emphasize here that I always use a spiritual approach. There is no vanity about being able to help others, because I know that it isn't my power, but God's love and power that makes any success possible. I just feel extremely grateful, and have come to realize that being able to do these things should not be my main goal in itself. These are all manifestations of spiritual development and evolvement, which is my true goal. It is all too possible to let these things become too important and get "stuck" in that phase and stop any further spiritual growth.

As time passed, I helped everyone who asked for my help. Eventually, I began to realize that people were asking me for help in situations which they should have handled themselves. If I helped them with these relatively minor things, how would they learn to cope with and solve the problems they were given for learning?

Eventually, I became more selective. I told people I would try to help them, only if they tried to deal with their problem and weren't able to resolve it. I encouraged them to use their minds as I did, knowing that we all had some ability to do this. Psychic ability is, in many ways, like any other talent. Some people are born to paint, sing, play an instrument, compose music, write books, poetry, and so on. We could all do these things to some extent with practice, but only those who have an inborn gift will excel in any of these areas.

The more I practiced going to an altered state of consciousness, (always praying when I got there), the more spiritual the whole process became. Soon, I began to be taken to many different places in the inner world, sometimes as an observer, sometimes as a participant in many ceremonies and rituals. I went to many beautiful places, and many wonderful things happened on these journeys, some of which I will relate later.

The most important result of all this was an increase in my love and devotion to God. There was also an increase in my appreciation of the complex and beautiful workings of the inner realm.

Probably as a result of the deep altered states in which I worked, I began to have outward manifestations of my spiritual progress. I cite many examples of this in the chapter entitled "Happenings".

While all these wonderful things were happening, my marriage was becoming more difficult. I decided that perhaps a divorce would be best for all concerned. When I suggested this to my husband, naturally he became upset. He said he felt it would harm the children and that we should try to work it out. I agreed to try and stayed for several more years, but was very unhappy with the relationship.

During these years, I did many things on the physical plane to take my mind off my marital situation. I talked my husband into our buying neglected houses in good areas, one at a time. With his excellent help, I would renovate them. After we finished one, we'd start on another. We lived in some of them while we did the required work. Usually, though, the houses were vacant while I worked on them. I spent many happy hours in them doing much of the physical labor myself. Stopping periodically, I would read and practice my metaphysical lessons and exercises at intervals.

One major thing I've learned these many years is that there is no end to this learning. As I said earlier, an answer to a question usually leads to more questions. Sometimes, what appear to be conflicting answers seem confusing, but cause me to really think! Often, I find more than one answer to the same question. Eventually, they both prove valid. We are given information according to our ability to comprehend it at the time. This information may change as our understanding grows.

# HEALING

In the following healing cases that I will describe, I want to impress on you that I am not seeking any accolades for my part in any of them. I tell of them only to demonstrate what God's power can do through us. I remind you, that I have no power of my own-only an intense desire to help others and I feel no self-pride when anyone is helped through me. What I do feel is gratitude that they have been helped and that I've been allowed to have a hand in it.

Healing isn't just for the body. It can be directed to any need a person may have. This need may be a relationship, career, finances, a mental condition, anything that can cause a real problem in a person's life.

I will write only of relatively few cases so that you may know the diversity and scope of the different types of problems, mainly physical, that are helped. I prefer to call what I do spiritual healing rather than psychic healing, because I approach all that I do from a spiritual aspect. Also, I want to emphasize that I never ask for or expect payment of any kind, because I feel I have so little to do with any of the help that people receive. However, when I lived in a different city after my divorce, I did accept a fee for metaphysical\spiritual counseling, but never for healing.

When I do a case, I ask to see the cause of the problem. I don't just want to know the symptoms, due to the fact that symptoms can be similar for various problems. When I work on situations, it is the same. I look for the cause of the problem and work on that. As I finish a case, I will always "see" a satisfactory result, thus bringing the creative forces into play.

Most of the cases I've done came to me because someone had heard about me from another person. I have never advertised my healing gift.

Some of the cases may seem unimportant to a casual observer, but may be causing the person who wants help a great

1

deal of concern. For instance, when one of my daughters was very young, she had a pretty face, but her ears stuck out and this bothered her. I suggested that each time she thought about them, instead of feeling upset about it, she should see her ears as she wanted them to be, to see herself looking in a mirror and liking the way her ears looked. At the same time, I also worked on her problem psychically, performing psychic "plastic surgery". Gradually, her ears did look the way she wanted them to look.

The power of the mind is unlimited. If we would remember to use this power positively, we could solve so many problems with much less stress and effort.

A different kind of problem follows. I had a phone call from a young lady one morning that said she wanted to see me right away. I asked her if she would like to make an appointment for the following day. I had a long list of activities scheduled that day unless an emergency came up. She replied that if I didn't see her right away, she was going to kill herself. Of course, I told her to come immediately! When she arrived at my house, I wanted to put her at ease, because she was very agitated. As we chatted, I mentally sent her peace and love. She started to tell me what her problem was. She was a lesbian and this had alienated her family and she was feeling very alone and had a poor self-image. As I began speaking with her, I sensed that her attention was being diverted. She mentioned that she had just come from the dentist, having had an extraction. The novocaine was wearing off, and she was in pain. I told her that until she could focus on what I would be telling her, I wouldn't be able to help her. We needed to remove the pain. She agreed, so I stood behind her and put my hands over her jaw and sent healing power into the painful area. In a few minutes, she asked me, "What did you do? The pain is gone." I replied that I had sent God's healing power into her. She had a look of amazement on her face and a look of trust and comfort. Now we could get to the real problem. As always, when counseling troubled people, I asked God to speak through me and I talked to the young woman for quite a while. When our session was over, she was greatly relieved of her previous agitation. She thanked me and said she wanted to learn to do what I did so that she could help others.

After reading about me in some articles that appeared in our local paper, a lady called me about her son who had been in a terrible auto accident. His brain was badly damaged, his spine was severed, and, for three years, he just sat and stared into space. He couldn't hear, taste, or smell, and could barely see. I worked on him immediately. His mother called me the next day to tell me what had happened the night before. He had been on the sofa with his parents. The TV was on and his mother changed the channel. He startled them completely by saying; "Do you think you're the only one watching that?" Needless to say, they were stunned to hear him speak. His physical abilities improved steadily. He was able to walk with the help of his parents. The doctors were amazed because they had said he'd always be a vegetable. He could talk, hear better than his parents, and see well enough to watch television. To my knowledge, however, he did not completely recover. This same lady had a brother who had cancer in every part of his body except his bone marrow and had only a few weeks to live. After I sent him healing, he could drive his car long distances and could do almost anything he was able to do before he became ill. She mentioned another brother who had been deaf in one ear for twenty-five years and wore a hearing aid. I sent him healing, removing a small bone from his ear psychically, and he no longer required a hearing aid. She also had a neighbor, an elderly man, who was dying. He made all those around him miserable because he was so angry and down right mean. She asked me to try to help him. I sent the healing energy to him and I was told he had died eventually but had become a very nice and agreeable person. God's power knew what was needed.

One day, a young man came to me asking if I could cause warts to go away. He had several on his hands. So I started to send healing to his hands, but as I did, I noticed he had a very bad case of acne too. Without saying anything to him, I also sent healing energy to that problem. I never saw or heard from him again, but someone who knew him saw him some time later and he had neither acne nor evidence that problem had ever existed. His skin was perfectly smooth. I can only assume the warts were gone as well!

Another day, a friend called to tell me her nephew in Mexico had a badly deteriorating spine. He had to be carried to his office in a hospital bed in a van and was in terrible pain. No one could help him. I went to work on him immediately, and psychically replaced all of his vertebrae and discs. My friend called later that same day to tell me he had actually been able to get up and had even gone to a wedding that evening and danced! This friend also had a little nephew in Mexico who made a whistling sound with every breath. They had taken him to several doctors, but they could find no cause for it. I checked him out with my mind and asked to see the cause. I was shown a small hole in his windpipe, which I repaired mentally, and he no longer "whistled".

This same lady had a son and daughter-in-law who were stationed in Germany. Her daughter-in-law had given birth to a baby and began hemorrhaging, and the doctors were unable to stop it. After several transfusions, my friend's son called his mother who asked for my help. I "saw" that her daughter-in-law's uterus was torn and "patched" it up. The bleeding then stopped. This same friend's third son's mother-in-law had exploratory surgery at a cancer center. The doctors found she had thousands of barnacle-type malignant tumors. They were match-head size, and clinging to all of her vital organs. The doctors closed the incision and gave the woman a couple of weeks to live. I went to see her at the hospital and used my hands to send her the healing energy. She "fell into a faint" and turned a healthy pink. The doctors were stunned at the change following this and dismissed her in a short time.

After a meeting one evening, a woman came up to me and asked if I would help her sister who lived in another city. The problem seemed to be that she had become withdrawn from the family. She was the youngest, and seemed to resent her sisters. No one could figure out why she felt as she did. I promised to do a reading as soon as I could, to call her to let her know what I had found out. During the reading, I was shown the younger sister as a little girl. She was trying to force her feet into a pair of black patent "baby doll" shoes. But she had out- grown them, and her sisters had taken them away from her so that she wouldn't hurt her feet. She cried and carried on and I finally got her to quiet down and asked her why she wanted to wear those shoes. She replied that because she was the baby of the family, her sisters often did not include her in their activities. Because these shoes looked like doll shoes, when she was wearing them she felt like a doll. Since little girls can imagine their dolls doing whatever they wished them to, she had spent many happy hours imagining herself doing things like her sisters did. When the shoes were taken away, these imaginary happy times were no longer possible for her. Consequently, she deeply resented her sisters. I explained to her that the shoes would have hurt her feet and her sisters weren't being "mean". They were actually thinking of her welfare because they loved her. I also explained that now that she was also grown up, she was able to do all these things she had imagined doing and didn't need any "magic" shoes. She seemed to be thinking of all of this and feeling better as I left her. I later called her sister and told her what had transpired in the reading. She in turn called her estranged sister who, hearing what the reading had revealed, began to cry and cried for a long time. There were no problems between her and her sisters after that.

At one time, there was a lot of intestinal flu in our town. So when my first husband began having the same symptoms, we thought that was his problem. After a day or two, instead of improving, he began to complain of severe abdominal pains. I immediately checked him out psychically, and saw that his appendix had burst! I called an ambulance at once and he was taken to the hospital. I told the doctor his appendix had burst and he asked me how I knew that. I told him I "just knew". My husband was examined and they operated immediately. While they were operating, I mentally projected myself into the operating room to help my husband with spiritual healing. When the doctor finished, he came out to talk to me and said if my husband hadn't been brought to the hospital when he was, most likely he wouldn't have survived. He told me my husband's abdomen was so full of "pus" that he had to put in three drains. During the night, I stayed at the hospital and worked on a spiritual level to drain all that poison out of his system. When the doctor came out of my husband's room the next morning, he was shaking his head and saying, "I don't understand it!". He then told me that he had expected there to be a great deal of drainage. But the bandages were clean and the abdomen was empty of pus. I just smiled, because I knew what had happened. My husband recovered in what I was told was an amazingly short time and was sent home to finish recuperating. After a day or two, he said he had a very bad backache. Again, I examined him with my mind to find the cause and was shown that the problem lay in his kidneys. They had a dry, leathery look, and when I "felt" them, they felt hard, almost crusty, but I saw the insides were still moist. I asked what this meant and the word "NEPHRITIS" was spelled out in front of me in big black letters. I had never heard this word before. I was also shown the treatment for it. I called the doctor and told him that I thought my husband had nephritis, and I "supposed" he'd subscribe such medication and treatment. He said that was correct and since my husband was diabetic this could have been very serious. He was put on the medication at once and recovered quickly.

A friend of mine who shared my interest in metaphysics was going to make several business stops in some small towns close by and asked if I'd like to come along. It would give us an opportunity to discuss the things in which we were both so deeply interested. As we traveled about, his car developed a radiator problem. While checking it out, he burned one of his thumbs severely. I put my hands around his thumb and went "within" to call upon God's healing power and sent it into his injured thumb. The pain stopped at once and later that day he called to tell me that it was completely healed-not even a blister! This same man stopped at my house one morning to ask my help for a friend of his who was outside in his car. She had just been stung on her leg by a wasp and said it was very painful. I put my hand over her leg and she jumped. She said it felt as if she'd been stung again, but the pain went away immediately and she was very relieved.

A reporter who had done a series of articles about me asked if I could help him with the pain in his legs. As he wasn't in my presence, I went "within" and asked to be shown the cause of his pain. I was shown that the chair he sat in to do his work did not fit him properly. The seat was too far from the floor, and, as a result, it was causing pressure on the backs of his thighs and impeding the circulation to his legs. I suggested that he put something under his feet to raise them enough so there wouldn't be any pressure on his legs. He did this and had no more problems with that condition.

Just a few days ago, one of my daughters had an accident in which her car was hit from behind. Her head hit her steering wheel very hard and she suffered a concussion. She felt so sick and confused at the site that she trusted the person responsible to write down his name and all pertinent information. There were no witnesses and she couldn't call the police because she felt so sick but managed somehow to drive home and call 911. The medic confirmed the fact that she had a concussion and told her how to treat herself. She tried to call the man who hit her car and found all the information he had given her was false. She then called me and was very upset because she would not be able to work for a few days. She's self-employed and would miss the money for work she had promised to do. This bothered her more than her injuries. Being her mother, I naturally sent healing to her injured head first and then programmed financial help for her. That same evening, someone stopped by to give her the same amount of money she would be losing by not working. They had not known of her accident but wanted to pay her in appreciation of something she had done for them without charge in the past. In two days all pain, swelling, and discoloration was gone from her head and there was no trace of her injuries.

One evening, I was visiting a friend and she said her husband was having a lot of pain in his lower back and asked me to see if I could find the cause. I went within my mind and saw that one of his legs was a little shorter than the other. I was given the information that he should put a lift inside the shoe on that foot. I was also able to tell him how thick the lift should be. He did this and had no more back pain.

My healing energy doesn't always work for people immediately. Often though the help will come soon in finding the right doctor, a new medication or in some other way. As long as they are helped, I am grateful and thank God for it.

I never tell people not to go to a doctor. On the contrary, I tell them to go if they need to. God works through doctors too! In fact, occasionally I took one of my children to their pediatrician if they did not respond quickly to healing and I felt that they needed medicine.

I remember one such time. I took one of my daughters to her doctor and told him what was wrong. He asked me how I knew and I told him. After examining her, he said I was right and prescribed the proper medication. He looked at me hesitantly and then said he had some patients that were ill and he couldn't find the cause and would surely like to ask me to check them out psychically. I told him I'd be most happy to do so and that I would keep it strictly between us, as I didn't even have to see the patient. Unfortunately, he never asked for my help. I've always regretted this but I can understand. I'm sure he was afraid that the medical community would somehow discover that he was working with a psychic and would take him to task for it.

Once in awhile, healing in absentia doesn't work. It is then necessary to actually see the person. One such case occurred when a friend asked me to send healing to her father who had, as she expressed it, "crumbling of the spine". He was in a "bent over" position and in "excruciating pain". He had gone to two or three doctors and was told that he would eventually be confined to a wheel chair and would have to wear a back brace. Even though he lived close by, I sent him healing "in absentia" several times. This made no difference in his condition. So I finally went to his house to see him. I asked him to lie on his stomach so I would have access to his back. It was very painful for him to get into this position. I held my hands close to his back in several places where I felt healing was needed. I did so until I felt he had absorbed the healing energy necessary to help him. I was told that night his back hurt him so badly he didn't think that he could stand it. But the next day his back was much better and continued to improve until he felt better than ever. His daughter told me later that ever since then he had done house building and yard work. He even climbed up a tree to saw off a branch that his son was unable to do because it was too hard for him.

This same friend's husband was experiencing severe pain under his heart. I checked him out immediately and found a hernia on the diaphragm, which I repaired psychically. She reported to me later that he had no more problems in this area.

Over a period of many years, I have formed some opinions about the different responses, or in some cases, the lack of response to the healing energies I send. I feel sure that when healing help does not occur, there are many possible reasons. One reason may be that the person may not want to be healed. This may be a conscious or unconscious desire. Perhaps they like the attention they get; perhaps it keeps families or spouses bound to them that they fear might otherwise leave. Perhaps it gives them an excuse from having to compete in the real world. It may even be an excuse for poor performance at home, at school or in the workplace.

Also, the attitude of people around them may affect them so either that they either do not accept healing or don't stay healed. They may constantly hear "Oh, he (or she) is always sick" or, "If there's an illness around, they'll get it". Other's attitudes can actually cause illness or prevent healing. Also, one's own attitude can certainly be a determining factor.

It could also be that, for some reason, a person has to have a certain condition until or unless they learn from it. Perhaps in a past life they were unsympathetic to someone with that particular difficulty and must now "walk in that person's shoes". Perhaps they don't feel "worthy" of being helped or just don't believe in spiritual healing and reject it. However, if at some level of being they truly want to be healed, they can often be helped.

Also, people are often helped who don't know someone is sending them healing energy. In fact, I sometimes recommend that certain people who might resist not be told. Thus, one might bypass the conscious mind that rejects help and contact the subconscious mind that may cooperate.

I must state again, here and now, that I never recommend that anyone not see a doctor. On the contrary, in a serious situation if the person isn't helped immediately, I always advise seeing a doctor, dentist, etc. Even if they are helped, I sometimes suggest that a physician check them out anyway. I believe that doctors and all people in the medical field are part of God's healing. Often, the healing energies will bring the patient the needed medical help. I am perfectly willing to continue to send healing under these circumstances.

By the way, I do not believe that healing needs to deplete the person sending the healing energy. In fact, I always feel wonderful after doing it. I wonder if those who feel tired after a healing session feel that they are the source of the energy instead of God. Since God is unlimited, there is always an unending supply of the proper amount of energy needed. It cannot be exhausted.

In the same vein, I never feel responsible if someone is or isn't healed or helped. When healing does occur, I am only grateful if I am the instrument through which they are helped.

# CLAIRAUDIENT EXPERIENCES

My first clairaudient experience occurred when I was in my late twenties. We were living in a new state and my husband's work took him away for several days at a time. I was often alone with my first child, who was about six years old, and our big German shepherd dog. I was pregnant and found it hard to sleep at times. One night, unable to sleep, I sat up in bed reading until the wee hours. Suddenly, I heard the sound of something being dragged across the floor of the attic just above me. I then heard a thump as if something had fallen. Not being the type to lie there and wonder about it, I decided to investigate. I couldn't figure out how anyone could have gotten past my open bedroom door and gone into the attic, since my big dog slept in front of the attic door outside of my room. She was extremely protective of us. I took the dog and a flashlight and went up into the attic to see what could have caused the noises. There was nothing up there and no way anyone could have gotten in from up there, so I just went back downstairs. A few weeks later we were entertaining guests who were from that area and just making conversation I mentioned this occurrence. They looked at me in a strange way and asked, "Don't you know the story about this house?" I replied that I didn't, since I was new in town and hadn't met any of my neighbors. They then told me that at one time the son of the family living in the house became very despondent and had gone into the attic, pulled a chair over to a rafter, put a noose around his neck, put the rope over the rafter and kicked the chair out from under him. This is what I had heard-a replay from a past unfortunate incident.

The second experience came shortly after this. I had given birth the night before and was awakened early in the morning by a woman's voice in the room across the hall from mine. She was obviously in trouble and calling in a quivery but loud voice for "Help" or "Hal". I couldn't quite tell which. After listening for some time and wanting to go back to sleep, I finally rang for a nurse. When she came in I asked her to please see to the woman across the hall because she needed help. The nurse gave me an odd look and blurted out, "There's no one in that room-she died this morning!" I knew nurses don't tell people that kind of thing, but I guess she was so shocked it just popped out!

On another occasion many years later, I had brought home a little brass bell and gave it to my youngest daughter to play with. After several minutes, the constant ringing began to get on my nerves and I took the bell and put it on a credenza in the foyer. I told her I didn't want her to play with it anymore that evening. We sat down to dinner and when she had finished eating, she asked to be excused and left the room. Shortly after, I heard the bell ringing again and I left the table to scold her for disobeying me. Much to my surprise, I found her sitting in the den absorbed in a TV program. I then went into the foyer and found the bell exactly where I had put it. I then realized "someone" was trying to get my attention. We had bought the house from an estate. The former owner had passed away and left it to her daughter from whom we had bought it. I had felt the former owner's presence at times and so had the children. It was a benign presence, so it didn't upset us. At any rate, I decided to use a ouija board to contact whomever it might be. (I didn't know at that time that I could contact and see entities through mental mediumship.) As I sat at the board, it spelled out a message for the former owner's daughter and her children. It gave the pet manes for her grandchildren, which, of course, we didn't know. I later contacted the daughter who came to see me and I gave her the message. (I had really wondered if it was authentic.) The daughter was very happy with the message and verified the names for her children.

I didn't use the ouija board after that. In fact, I disposed of it because I didn't want my children to use it as a toy. I had already cautioned them that they could have problems if they tried to use one. Of course, I had always invoked spiritual protection before I began.

All of my children display psychic ability in some form. All are super sensitive, as I am, to feelings of other people and to their own feelings in relationships with others. This is a blessing, which can feel more like a curse at times.

My oldest daughter is an accomplished artist and writer and has a lovely singing voice. My second daughter sings, composes music and plays several instruments. My third daughter is also artistic, sings and entertains and writes lovely poetry. My fourth daughter also draws, writes beautiful poems and gives psychic readings for her friends. My fifth daughter plays different instruments and teaches music. All of these gifts, I believe, are psychic gifts. When they are functioning in their various activities, I firmly believe that they are mentally in a state of altered consciousness. This is especially true if they are in a creative mood.

# EXPERIENCES AT LEVEL

When I first began doing metaphysical work, I had made a practice of worshiping God when preparing to do cases. When I first began this, I had envisioned an altar with a tabernacle with gold doors. One day, I was told to "Come unto Me", and I entered into the tabernacle into the most beautiful light, and a feeling of utter bliss and peace filled me. I did not want to leave this place, but I knew I must as I had many cases to do. However, I was most happy to find this experience repeated each time I prepared to do my daily cases until it finally became unnecessary, because I began to feel the light and state of bliss whenever I went to an altered state of consciousness.

One morning as I approached my mental place of worship, I saw a woman standing before the altar. Her back was to me. I noticed she had very long, beautiful dark brown hair. She was wearing a simple light brown garment that reached just below the calf of her legs. As I stared at her, she turned around and I was struck by her beauty. Such peace and goodness was radiating from her! I said to myself, "If I were perfect, I would look like that!" I did not know it at the time, but I had just met the female aspect of that part of God within myself!

I had read many times about people who had spiritual guides that helped them and worked through them. I thought it would be wonderful to have one too, and prayed very hard for this to happen. It didn't seem to happen, so I continued to pray. Day after day, I beseeched God to send me a spirit guide to work through me. Finally, one day, a voice within me said, "Why do you need them when you have me?" I knew then that it was Jesus' voice and I felt no need for any other guide after that.

Many years later while doing cases, I noticed a figure off to my right, but I did not pay a lot of attention to it because I was absorbed in the case I was doing. The figure continued to appear whenever I did cases, and one day started to move closer and I

17

recognized Jesus! I said to Him, "Please, I'm not ready for this!" Hearing His voice was fine, but actually seeing Him was overwhelming! I felt too unworthy for Him to come to me, but He stayed there, saying nothing and, gradually, as the days went by, I accepted His presence, still feeling a sense of wonder. He continued to be there, giving me his support and love.

When I initially began communicating with beings on the inner planes, I knew when God spoke to me because I would see no one. All the other communications were from beings I could see. I always called this voice from the unseen being the "voice of God." One day, this voice gave me a name to call Him and I was shown how to spell it. I felt uncomfortable about this and gave it many tests, but finally realized that I had been blessed with a special name to call God. He told me that this name was a combination of our vibrations and I understood that each of us would have a different "private" name for Him because each of us had vibrations peculiar to us only. No two were alike. This was to prepare me for later revelations and experiences.

After a long time, I was communicating on the inner planes and saw a patriarchal figure, very majestic, with gray hair and beard. He was dressed in a long robe with every imaginable color in it in a diamond pattern. Each diamond shape was about two inches high and one inch across on a dark background. The neck, sleeves and hem were bordered with a wide, dark band with a gold scroll-type pattern similar to what I would call a Greek key design. He appeared to be standing in a gentle breeze. I asked him who he was and he gave me the name I had been given to call God! This was not acceptable to me, because I knew no one could see God. I told him, "They say no one can see God.", and He replied, "But they do not know Me!". He kept appearing every time I went to an altered state of awareness. Again, I gave every test that I could think of, but He remained and I finally came to accept Him. He explained to me then that He had assumed a physical appearance so that we might have a closer, more personal relationship. Let me make it clear that I do not claim that this is the image God would assume to appear to anyone else. It was only because I had this "Father image" about God that He chose this form to present to me. In fact, when I see him now, He is much younger and dresses differently. God will choose to appear in any form that a person will find acceptable.

He continued to be with me, and after I became accustomed to His presence, one day I noticed an ethereal female figure, almost transparent, visible from the shoulders up, emerging from his head and shoulders. Each day, this figure emerged more until the entire female form became visible. At first, she continued to be almost transparent. I could just detect that this was a female form clad in long, flowing robes and wearing a veil over her head. Her garments, too, were fluttering in a gentle breeze. Finally, she became a solid figure and stood beside Him. I was made to understand that this was the female aspect of God, equal in every way to the male aspect. Then, I remembered the Biblical account of the creation of Adam and Eve, "In His own likeness He created them, male and female He created them." Thus, it was made clear to me about the dual nature of God.

Then, a strange thing began to happen as the days went by. God's male self stayed a little behind as the female self came closer, and I understood that while God is complete in both aspects within each of us, it is the female aspect which acts primarily in women and the male aspect in men. Both are always present in us and we can call upon God for all our needs at all times and either aspect responds, depending on the situation.

Looking back at the time my dear friend Jesus had first appeared to me, I realized that He had come to lead me to God within myself and that is also why He came to earth-to bring us to the realization of God's presence within us, not some far off place in the sky.

Ever since the day God's dual nature was made so clear to me, I pray to "Mother-Father" God, giving my full attention and love to the total God, not to just the male part as I had been taught to do.

It had been impressed upon me in my meditations that the human race cannot evolve fully spiritually until both aspects of God are accepted. It had also been impressed upon me that women in general should be given their rightful place as equal to men. This is not "across the board" equality because there are differences. But all must come to realize that women's contributions are of equal importance in the overall scheme of things. Of course, it is my personal opinion that if a woman can do the same jobs as a man in the workplace, and do it as well, then she should receive equal pay and opportunities. By the same token, if a man chooses to do something that is traditionally "woman's' work", he should not be looked down upon. Everyone should be free to do what he or she does best, whether or not it is "traditional".

I have been told that in my next lifetime, it will be my life's work to teach about God's dual nature. I am to help people to understand how very important it is to recognize that men and women are equal in God's eyes, each in their own unique way. All this is a must for utmost spiritual growth and evolution to a higher plane of consciousness. I realize that these things will be very much opposed by many men and even some women, but eventually all will and must accept this.

Several years after my first husband and I were divorced, I was at level and was shown a man who would be my "next" husband. I had no intention of marrying again. I planned to retire at the end of that year and move to Mexico. I had visited there at one time and loved the Guadalajara area. I planned to live there very simply and help the poor Mexican people by sending healing energy into any who came to me for that reason. However, I thought it would be interesting to see what I would be shown. I saw a man's face and then a speeding freight train coming right at me, and I was made to understand the symbolism of this-when I met this man I would be "swept off of my feet", and nothing would stop us from being together, and it would happen soon. I met him a few months after I was shown this and we were married within a month. Obviously, I wasn't supposed to go to Mexico!

As I've shown, some things are presented to me in symbolic forms at times, and one day, I had an amusing experience. I found myself (at level) in a place that resembled a library, except the aisles of books were endless. The shelves were so tall I couldn't see the tops. As I looked about me in utter amazement, an old man approached me. He resembled pictures I had seen of Father Time. He told me I was in "the Hall of Records" where everyone's lives were kept track of and registered. He asked me if I'd like to see mine, and I replied I surely would! He showed me a huge volume that had only one page left to fill out, and I said, "Oh, good! This will be my last time on earth!". He looked at me and dryly replied, "We can always start a new book!" What I was being shown and told was that I could "screw up" and have to come back again!

As I started to do cases one day Jesus came into view and approached me. I was sitting down and He knelt in front of me so he could look directly into my eyes and asked me, "Will you take my place on earth?" I was so stunned I couldn't answer at first. Finally, I said, "How could I possibly do such a thing?" But He continued to stare into my eyes and just repeated the question. After doing my cases, I came back to a normal state of consciousness and pondered this. I finally decided He most likely meant to help people as I was doing and live according to his teachings. Now I feel that he might have been referring to my next life in which I've been told I would teach and heal and do other things with God's power so people would pay attention to my message. I feel very unworthy of the honor He bestowed upon me by coming to me as He did and am determined to do my best to emulate Him.

One day as I was at level preparing to do cases, I saw myself sitting on a chair. A beautiful little boy who looked about two years old came and put his elbows on my knees and gazed into my face. He had very big, blue eyes and a head full of golden curls. I asked him who he was, and he said he was the baby I had lost (miscarried) who would have been born between my third and forth daughters. I was so delighted to have him with me and he was there for quite a long time-many weeks. One day, he came to me and said he had come to say good-bye. I asked him where he was going, and he replied, "I'm going to be born." Two years later, I saw a picture of my grandson and it was the little boy who had come to me during meditation.

As I was meditating another time, I was told "You are the first of the new race." When I came back to an "everyday awareness" level, I pondered on this. Why had I, of all the billions of people, past and present, been chosen for this high honor? As I mused on this, I realized that what was meant was that I was a prototype. There are many of us on the earth-I am not unique. Eventually, all humanity will learn to use their minds as I do and thus, the new race would come into being.

I have enjoyed reading about Carl Jung who originally was influenced by Freud, but then came into his own way of thinking. So many of his experiences have been similar to mine that I felt a real kinship. After reading some books by and about him, I asked a professor friend of mine to recommend some other books Jung may have written. He did so, and I obtained the books that were more technical than I expected. I was wondering how on earth I'd understand them and suddenly, a figure of an old man appeared to me in my mind. He said to me, "I'll help you." I asked him who he was and he said, "I'm Carl Jung." Apparently, he did just as he said he would. I was reading a very involved chapter in one of his books and said to myself, "This isn't correct-it should be like this!" I wrote out what I thought would be the correct version, complete with diagrams. Then, I called my professor friend and explained what

I had read and my correction of it. He replied that Carl Jung had made the same correction in his next book!

One year, on the date of my birthday, I was working on the inner planes when I went through a birth process and finally came "into the light". A week or so later, again at level, I became the Phoenix, reduced to ashes. Out of the ashes I emerged as a larva, which turned into a white dove, the symbol of the Holy Spirit. It was made clear to me that this is the part of God I am expressing.

The Holy Spirit is not the primal energy (I was told) which is the Father, nor the creative energy, which is the mother. The Holy Spirit is the "doer" that which acts upon what the creator has used the power to produce. Shortly after this, I received a pair of white dove figurines.

The next experience was, as so many are, symbolic, telling me what was happening in another way, on another level. This concerns a young man that I will mention again in the chapter titled "Walk-Ins". We were in a UFO operating room. Metal hoods were placed on our heads. They put two suction-cup-like discs on our foreheads with tubes and cups on either end. They then took the tube from my forehead and attached it to his and did the same with a cup and tube from his forehead. They then put a tube from my arm into his (below the shoulder) and some of my blood went into his. I was told this was so some of "their" blood would get into his. I asked them why they didn't give him their blood directly and they replied because they were not in physical bodies and I was "one of them". This was all symbolic of the actual happening on this level. I was teaching him much of what I knew and sharing with him many things as I experienced them. This was putting new thoughts into his head and making him more aware of the unseen world. In this way, he was being prepared to be "one of us".

One morning as I was saying my prayers before arising, I was greeting Jesus and His Mother. I noticed how blue His eyes were. I think perhaps His eyes are supposed to be brown, but I always see them as a beautiful sky blue. As a teenager in a Catholic high school, we were asked to compose a Christmas poem during English class. I remember a couple of lines from it:

"So softly glow His bright blue eyes.

Surely He came from Paradise."

I don't remember the rest of the poem, but I do remember the nun asking if I had actually made it up, or if it was from a book. At any rate, even then I visualized them as blue. As I looked into His eyes on the morning I speak of above, they seemed to be coming toward me and getting larger and larger. Finally, they enveloped me and I was inside them. As Jesus drew away from me, He said, "I have given you my essence; I have given you the core of Me. You now have the Christ mind." This just amazed me and I pondered over it all day. When I lay down to rest later, I went to level to ask Him questions about it. I said, "I didn't know a Christ-mind could be given to someone. I thought each of us had to earn it!" He replied, "You have earned it!" (So this was a symbolic ritual!) I felt I was a long way from this state of being, and I was filled with wonder. (I still am!) When I asked if this would change me in any way, He said, "You'll see!" I didn't feel any different, except that I was filled with awe and delight. For some reason, I then recall being shown my "twin" soul a long time before this. He had beautiful sky-blue eyes, and I was told, "By his eyes you will know him." Was there any connection? What did it all mean? As usual, I was confused! I decided to meditate on all this until I understood it. As soon as this thought came to me, I was told, "What is there to understand? Just accept it. It is done!"

# THOUGHTS AND REVELATIONS

I have meditated many times on why and how we are on the earth. What follows is one train of thought that came to me many years ago.

I definitely believe that most of us who incarnate on earth are "fallen angels" who are working our way back to our former state. Every time we discover a "new" truth, we are actually being allowed to "remember" this truth and these things are revealed to us in stages, as we are ready. Angels are our guardians and helpers and it is an individualized aspect of God within us that directs and guides us. We are allowed to start back on the path, as our consciousness becomes ready. Perhaps those who are "old souls" and some that have become "Masters" were less guilty than others and were allowed to come back sooner than some others who were more directly involved in the "Rebellion". Thus, the difference in awareness and behavior in various people.

I have an answer to these musings in the following chapter.

# REINCARNATION

One of the most difficult concepts for me to accept was reincarnation. I had been brought up to believe that death was final, that we would be judged immediately and would end up in one of three places: The really good souls went to Heaven. The souls who were in need of a bit more understanding of their shortcomings were sent to Purgatory, which may have been like Hell, but one didn't stay there forever. The really bad souls went to Hell for eternal damnation and torment. Oh, yes, all unbaptized babies went to Limbo where they were happy, but could never see God. Even as a child, this didn't seem fair to me.

As I studied metaphysics, again and again reincarnation was mentioned. I even read whole books on the subject, but I didn't accept it. Even after I began to use God's power for healing and helping, I did not accept it. I fought the very idea of it for at least three years after I began doing readings on health and other situations.

I had always asked to see the cause of a condition or situation rather than the symptoms, and, every now and then, I was shown a past life of the individual involved. In that past life, the person I was working with had done something or not done something that, in turn, had caused their current problems. I began to consider the possibility that reincarnation just might enter into our present difficulties. Especially was this finally brought into my awareness when I realized that everything else I was shown or told proved to be correct. Why would this one thing be in error? I puzzled over this for a long time and finally decided it was the only logical conclusion. I thought, "If God is fair and just, and I know this is true, why would a fair and just God allow "unfair things" to happen? Why were some people born under such different circumstances and experience such different lives and all are expected to arrive at the same level of goodness and awareness in one life? Where is the justice of a child born to good parents, perhaps beautiful and intelligent and so on; being compared equally with a child born under adverse circumstances such as cruel or uncaring parents, or perhaps deformed or defective in some way? Why should a person subjected to terrible events be compared to one whose life was fairly stable and pleasant? Why were these differences permitted?"

I had been told by my teachers and clergy that God had a special love for these unfortunate people if they bore their suffering bravely and did not complain. Thus, they would gain a special place in Heaven. Again, I wondered what was fair about that!

On and on went the question until I finally realized that we must all be given every opportunity for salvation. After all, if our soul is part of God, and God cannot be destroyed, then how could our souls be destroyed? Only through repeated lives could a soul finally learn what to do and what not to do and act upon this knowledge. They would do this not because of fear of damnation, but because the soul finally realizes that the love for God, total commitment to God, was the reason for it's existence. When souls finally reach this state of being, they are ready to become full co-creators with God. The more I thought of the theory of reincarnation, I realized that if people accepted it they would not ask God, "Why me?" when they had problems. Also, if people understood that they had been or would be (probably) all races and both sexes in their many lives, they would be more understanding of other people.

At any rate, I began doing a past life reading for myself. I asked about my marriage. It was not a happy one because, as is so often the case, my husband wanted to dominate me. At first, I had accepted this but felt, as I grew older, that I was entitled to be myself. In this reading, I was shown a past life in the early days of this country during the time the West was being settled. My husband in that life treated me like a possession, a chattel. This same being was my first husband in this life. I was expected to remain quiet unless a question was directed at me, to never complain, no matter how hard my life might be. It was necessary in my present life to break that pattern. My husband had to accept me as a partner in marriage, not just as someone who was there for his convenience. I had to express my individuality, to insist on being recognized as a person in my own right. I had known the first time I saw him in this life that we would be married. I know now that we were brought together to work out our "Karma" from that past life.

He also had a tendency in this life to ridicule my metaphysical work. This led me to ask in another reading why, if I was to do this work, did he seem to try to make it more difficult? I was shown a weight lifter. As soon as he could manage to lift a weight, more was added to it so it was again an effort. I was told, "Without opposition, you cannot grow strong."

My middle daughter (#3) came into this life with a "chip on her shoulder" towards me. I had really wanted this child and had planned to give her a lot of extra attention. Since my second child was almost 12 years of age I'd have time to devote to a new baby. I bought a big old-fashioned wooden rocker, enameled it white and bought a pad for the seat and back. I intended to spend many happy hours in it, rocking that baby, singing to her, telling her stories, and so on. Much to my dismay, she wouldn't even let me hold her unless I carried her around and showed her objects I thought would interest her.

If I tried to hold her to give her a bottle, she'd stiffen out like a little board and wouldn't eat. I had to put her in her crib or buggy and prop the bottle while I stood by to make sure she wouldn't choke on it. My second daughter became like a mother to her when she was at home. The baby let her hold her, feed her, and so on. When she could talk and I tried to dress her, she'd pull away and say, "Don't touch me!" Naturally, I felt confused and hurt by her attitude because I loved her so and wanted to hug and cuddle her. One day, I asked her why she was so angry with me all the time. She gave me two answers. (She was just three years old at the time.) She said, "You don't love me." and, "You didn't make me a boy." I was aware that she didn't like being a girl. She hated wearing dresses and only wanted to wear jeans, cowboy boots and hats and act like a boy. (I'm happy to say that she changed into a most attractive young lady who enjoyed "being a girl"!

Her childhood desire to be a male was explained in the following past life reading that I did when I realized I had the ability to do it. In that life, I was living in the Deep South in the antebellum era. I saw myself sitting under a spreading tree wearing a very full-skirted dress which billowed about me. There was a pretty wide-brimmed hat on the grass beside me. As I sat there, a handsome young man came riding up on a horse, got down and came to me. He began trying to coax me to allow him to court me, but I was only amused. This had happened many times, and each time I had told him that I wasn't interested. I loved someone else and planned to be married. I knew the rejected young man was now my daughter in this life, thus the feeling she had that I didn't love her. This reading also explained why she had wanted to be a boy when she was little and hated wearing dresses until she was a teenager. She also loved horses, which led to our owning several.

In another reading for the two of us, I saw myself in a harem. I was the first wife of the man I was married to, but he had several others. My daughter was the newest wife. Because she was young and beautiful, he enjoyed her company. She felt she should replace me. However, I was his companion and confidant and he would spend most of his time with me. In a fit of jealous rage, she tried to kill me with a dagger. This reading explained some of the animosity that she felt toward me. It also helped to explain why I was not quite comfortable if a sharp knife was visible. I put them away as soon as I finished using them. When I shared this reading with her, it seemed to help our relationship and things are fine between us now. I tell you of this particular case in such detail to show how past lives can affect the present one.

Another time, I asked to see past lives of my own. In one, I was a priestess in ancient times. I wore a feather headdress and was in a cave with a crude stone altar lit with a flickering flame on either side. As I stood in front of the altar, a man and a woman came in. She was carrying a new baby and held it out to me. As I looked on this scene, I felt so elated. I thought I was a healer way back then and they were bringing their baby to me to heal it of some kind of problem. Imagine my utter horror when I saw myself remove the baby's heart in some kind of ritual and devour it! I came out of the altered state instantly, totally shocked and disgusted. I still felt so later when I went back and asked the meaning of this despicable performance. I was told that it was an honor for these parents to have their baby chosen as a sacrifice to their gods. I still feel revulsion as I recall that scene.

Another time, I was shown a life as a little boy in surroundings that reminded me of biblical times. I was a homeless waif in that life and died at an early age of starvation.

Later, I was shown myself again in male form, as a teenager in the Civil War. (This life must have happened rather soon after the antebellum one.) There was a very cruel, sadistic man in charge of the unit I was in and he picked on me constantly. I was shown a scene where he made me dig a deep hole and then get in it. Only my head was above ground. It was raining and cold and the hole filled with water, but I was afraid to get out. (I was being punished for a very minor offense.) In that lifetime I died of pneumonia as a result of that particular act of cruelty.

Later, in thinking about this, I wondered if that lifetime had left its mark on me in problems I've experienced with my health in this lifetime. As a child, I had severe respiratory problems and was not expected to live. As an adult, I was subject to pneumonia several times and still have respiratory problems, which are gradually improving.

As I thought of the many past lives we all must have had, I wondered how we all got so messed up in the first place that we had so much to learn. The following information was given to me:

"When God created the angels, they were given the ability to use God's power just as God did; to create and manifest. Eventually, some angels began to think this power was their own, not from God, but from within themselves. They began to draw away from their Creator, which led finally to an open rebellion. They were, of course, defeated and could no longer remain in Heaven. They could not be destroyed, because they were part of God. They had to be sent to places where they could start their way back. Earth was one such place. This earth is the "Hell" where they would learn and experience. It was a place of trial, and since their error in thinking was such a serious one, it would take many lives to work things out."

It is also my understanding that the more influential an angel had been in leading others in the revolt, the more learning was necessary to work their way back. I was told that all souls born into a body on earth had been "fallen angels" with very few exceptions. Jesus was an outstanding exception through whom God spoke and acted, to help "lost souls" find their way back.

# ANGELS AND US AND SEPARATION

Being curious about some of the beings that interacted with me on the various inner planes, I asked if they were "multidimensional". They replied that they were "ultra-dimensional", beyond dimension, unrestricted so they could go anywhere, whenever they were needed or could be of use. These, of course, are the angels who are ready to help us always.

I have come to believe that there are angels in charge of all things. We can work together with them for our mutual benefit and the benefit of humanity. For instance, I believe there is an angel in charge of all animal life and underlings in charge of each type of animal. For instance, all canines have their own angel, all felines, birds, fish, even insects in charge of a guardian spirit for their particular species. I had read different things to this effect, but now I understand the angelic hierarchy so much better.

It is my understanding that the Supreme Deity created angels to carry out the work. They serve as liaisons between God and all things. As we evolve, we are not only able to understand this but use this knowledge to accept our own proper roles. We are truly unlimited, as we are one with God. Our minds are one with the Creative Force. The more we realize this, the more we share the power. We are limited only because we accept limitations.

Those who use this power in wrong ways limit themselves because the source of the power is all-good. The more we use the power for good, the more godlike we become and the more power is available to us.

While reading "A Course in Miracles" some time ago, the following came to me: God made us in His own image and likeness, co-creators with Him. But, in our pride and arrogance, we began to think it was our power, separate and apart from God and, as a result, we felt separated. Thus, "sin" was born. Now, we must regain realization of who and what we really are.

We felt guilty about our separation and thus created the ego to continue the farce of separation. We are the "fallen angels"; almost all of us born into bodies on this earth. This earth is the "hell" we were cast into, to live our lives over and over until we finally realize our true nature. It has been a division, which exists only in our minds, not God's. We cannot really be separated from God or "lost" or damned to an eternal hell, as God is part of us and God cannot be lost or destroyed.

Over the years, I've done several readings on angels and "The Fall", the rebellion in Heaven after which those who rebelled were "cast out".

This particular reading was done in July 1985.

"In the beginning, we were all one, a happy, joyous family, co-creators with God and you were one of us. Then, discontent set in, a feeling of boredom, wanting to be more and do more. You began misdirecting the energy away from Me (God). You did then and still do have freedom of choice. Instead of using the abilities to broaden the good that was possible, you and others directed it to rebellion, and we became foes. The irony was that you would have become more instead of less had you remained. You left us, you were not "cast out", and as you grew further away from us, your desire to be different crystallized and you became so, using your abilities in negative ways and creating that which you could control for your own purposes. Thus was "evil" born into realization and exists so even today. Some of you at last became contrite and asked to be permitted to return. This permission was granted, and you began the long trek back, which you have just completed. You were not a leader but a follower, and thus not as removed as some, but even so it has taken myriads of lifetimes in many forms to accomplish this. Your feeling that all born into a form on the earth were rebellious angels is correct, but not only on earth is this true. On this earth, you made your progression through many forms, even those inanimate, and experienced the lowest self-realization possible, even as a stone, being a form of coagulated energy, for that is how far removed you were from a being of light that you

34

had been. You have been a part of all nature, plants, animals, even clouds, and as human forms became available, you then were permitted to enter into these. You have been truly earthbound since you decided to come back but, in between earth visits, you have had experiences in the spirit on other planets, mostly in this part of the universe and, indeed, in this galaxy. Venus has been your favorite place of respite, but you have been on all the planets that revolve around "your" sun."

Even as I read these words so many years later, I am amazed. Apparently, we are not limited to visible forms, but perhaps also invisible forms, even energy patterns we are not aware of here on earth.

Another short reading about "Fallen Angels".

"Yes, they were on earth in human form in the earliest stages, but life was very difficult and short and they rebelled against it. Some, separately, some in groups, but all resisted being born again. It was necessary to come here to progress in those days because of the very unevolved quality of the human mind. There was no choice until a certain amount of intellect was acquired."

There are many angels who help me to help others. I had a very personal experience with one. My husband and I had gone out to dinner, leaving my fourteen-year-old daughter in charge of her two younger sisters. When we came home, I noticed that the inside lights of my car were on and the driver's side door was slightly ajar. I had left my car in the garage and I knew I hadn't left it like that. When I tried to shut the door, it wouldn't close and I noticed it was dented! I knew for sure it hadn't been that way when I left, so I asked my daughter what had happened. She told me she had decided to take my car for a little drive to a nearby city. Now, she was just learning to drive and we had told her she was not to drive unless one of us was with her and I had hidden the extra key to insure that she couldn't! The accident had happened when she was turning to go under an overpass to come back home. She had turned in front of another car, which couldn't avoid hitting her. Fortunately, the people who had hit my car were very nice about it and the man drove my car to our house and his wife drove my daughter home. The police had given my daughter a ticket and she had to go to court. I felt it was so unfair for my husband and me to be penalized when we had done everything we could to keep her from driving. Now we, as her parents, would have to pay a fine. So I went "within" and asked that there would be no fine for us and I visualized coming home from court and telling my husband this. On the appointed day, I took my daughter to court and we sat there for a long time as person after person went before the judge. At one time, I thought he called her name, but the people around us were talking and I wasn't sure. I suggested she go up and ask, but she said she would be too embarrassed if he hadn't called her name. Just then, a small, young black man walked up to the bench. I sat back-and we waited and waited for her name to be called. Finally, we were the only ones left and the judge asked us what we wanted. I explained that we were supposed to come that day and gave him the information. He went through the papers he had and said hers weren't there. Finally, he suggested we go to where the fines were paid and we found her fine had been paid! This caused some confusion at first, and then the judge said, "I remember this. A young black man had come up and I asked him if he was (gave my daughter's name) and he said he was. Then, I asked him if he lived at your address, and he said yes, he did, and paid the fine-$200.00!" I thought at the time that this was strange because there were no black people living in the community! He said that since the fine was paid we owed nothing. When I got home, my husband asked me how much it had cost us and I said to him, "Nothing". I told him what had happened. He had a puzzled look, but didn't say anything, but I knew that one of my angel friends had helped me!

One day when I was doing cases, I noticed another black angel among my angel friends. He came forward and said he was there to help me with special cases. This was made very clear to me on the day a friend called. She was very frightened and was calling from a pay phone. She had been driving through a black community when a car driven by an elderly black man had gone past a stop sign and hit her car. She said he was very upset and was shouting at her and saying it was her fault. A crowd was gathering and she felt threatened. I told her I'd go to level immediately and did so while she was still on the phone. I was told by my friends on the inner plane that all would be well. So I told her not to worry, it would be all right. She went back to her car and the crowd came closer. Suddenly, a huge black man appeared and began talking to them. He quickly calmed them down and then the police came. She looked around for her rescuer to thank him, but couldn't see him anywhere. This puzzled her because there was no place for him to go so quickly. They had been in the middle of the intersection and there was not even a tree close by. When she related all this to me later, I knew my black angel friend had heard the problem and had helped.

In a lighter vein-I was at a mall and had been looking for a parking place and, after driving up and down, lane after lane, I finally asked my angels to please help me. Suddenly, I saw a figure ahead of me beckoning to come forward and turn down a lane at his left. I did, and found a parking place immediately. Since then, I always ask my angels to find me a good parking place and I always do. I always also remember to thank them for their help.

They also help me to find my car if I forget where I've parked it!

Excerpt from an old reading of mine:
"Angels do not help God! They help humanity. God needs no help! God created some angels to do certain things, to carry out His plan-they are His intermediaries; through them, He does His work-not because He needs it done through them, but because they love doing it."

37

This sounds a bit confusing, but I know that certain angels are assigned certain tasks and their happiness lies in doing what they were created to do.

# THOUGHT FORMS

Thoughts are things-they have an energy and sensitives can pick them up at times. When you think of a person or a place, part of you goes to that person or place. I will give examples of this from my own experience.

At one time, I was visiting another psychic healer and his wife in Ohio. He had invited several people over to meet me one night. As they came into the room, I "saw" another man enter with them, and when they were all seated, this figure leaned against the wall very casually next to one of the men. My host knew I had sensed something that the group might like to hear about. I mentioned the "thought form" I could see very plainly, and described his appearance to the man he'd come with. That man said he didn't know who it was, so I asked the thought form who he was. He gave me a first name, which I do not recall. At any rate, the guest still didn't know who he was and said; "I don't know anyone like that". At this, the form became exasperated and shouted (which only I could hear, of course) "The hell you don't; we talk almost every day on the phone!" I relayed this message to the guest who said "Oh, yes, now I know who he is, but I seldom see him. We do a good deal of business, but mostly over the phone!" This exchange rather amazed the other guests.

On another occasion, I was in Little Rock, Arkansas, to attend a seminar given by Harold Sherman at a local hotel. I had gone there with a friend and we had both taken our little dogs along. We were looking forward to the evening's program. There would be a dinner after which the featured guest was to be Jean Dixon. I decided to take the dogs for a little walk before dinner. I got on the elevator to go back to my room. Imagine my pleasure at seeing Jean Dixon on the elevator. I smiled at her and she smiled back at me and I thought how considerate the few other passengers were not to be staring at her and whispering, etc. I left the elevator and went to our room and told my friend about seeing Miss Dixon. We went to dinner really looking forward to an interesting evening. Imagine my shock when Mr. Sherman got up to speak and said he was sorry to tell us that Jean Dixon had been delayed and couldn't get there until the next day! I had seen her "thought form" since she must have been thinking about not being able to be there. In doing so, she had projected a very solid image of herself there and I had picked it up! At any rate, we had a most enjoyable time at the dinner that evening. Afterwards, some of us were standing in a group discussing various subjects. There were perhaps ten or twelve of us in that particular group and we got to mentioning our astrological signs. Much to our surprise, every one of us was a Virgo! Birds of a feather! I mention this episode just to emphasize the kind of things that can occur when like-minded people gather together.

Getting back to thought forms-at first, I couldn't distinguish between a thought form and a discarnate because they looked the same to me-a definite personage, but usually not quite solid. (Jean Dixon was an exception.) It was usually only while communicating with them that I would find out which they were.

When my friend and I made our plans to go to the above seminar, we had both used our minds to visualize a safe trip by "seeing" the car surrounded by the Christ light. But prior to this trip, my friend had thought of making another trip and had asked me to check out if it would be a safe trip. I did so and saw her driving down a road and a red pickup truck coming off a side road and crossing right in front of her. She later decided not to take that trip. At any rate, on the way home from our seminar, we were going down the highway at about 60 m.p.h. when a red pickup truck pulled out from a side road on our right and crossed the highway directly in our path. My friend swerved the car into a farm driveway on our left and screeched to a stop. The red pickup truck had also pulled into this driveway. Apparently, the man driving in it lived there. My friend shouted at him, "Mister, do you know you almost killed us?" He replied in a slow drawl, "Well, I put my hand out to turn in here!" Later, we realized the dark humor in this remark.  We also realized that in spite of everything, our car's actions had been smooth.  Even breaking to a quick stop, not a drop of coffee had spilled from our two full cups.  We had seemed to float in a big, soft bubble.  Later, when we came to a gradual stop for a train, the coffee spilled all over!  The Christ Light had protected us.  The "almost" accident mentioned above was obviously the potential accident I had seen for her in that earlier reading.

# SEEING DISCARNATES, HAUNTINGS, ETC.

As a child, I was afraid of seeing something that would frighten me. Not monsters and so on, as most children are frightened of, but discarnates, or, as I called them then, "spooks". I remember going to bed and pulling the covers over my head with just my nose sticking out so I could breathe and I would pray, "Please God, don't let me see anything that will scare me." Even when I grew up, I still was uncomfortable about the possibility of seeing something frightening and I did not want this to happen!

However, after I learned to help people by using my mind and God's power, I decided perhaps I could help people if I functioned as a medium. I actually experimented with becoming a medium by making my voice, body and so on available to a spirit who might desire to communicate through me. After one such experience, which left me feeling disoriented, I asked God if I might, instead, "see" them and communicate as I would with a living person. I was told that this was certainly all right. I then began to see and communicate with them without fear. This was preferable, as I could do this whether or not there were other people present, but usually, others were present. I also began seeing thought forms about this time. Actually, I think they may both be the same, only thought forms are from living people, and discarnates are from people who have "passed over" to the other side. In each case, they are projecting their thoughts and image to us and sometimes energy in other forms as well.

For instance, an apartment manager called to ask if I could help her daughter. She and her husband were living in one of the apartments, and there had been strange and frightening things going on there, all seemingly electric in nature. Lights would go off and on, appliances and the vacuum cleaner turned off and on by themselves, and so on. Her daughter and her husband were terrified. A friend asked if he could accompany me, so we went that night to do what I could to help. As soon as I went "within",

I could see an ugly, dark, red and black cloud swirling and spinning and filling the whole room. In the middle of it, I saw a man, a woman and a girl who looked to be about twelve years of age. Then, I "saw" the man beating his wife and she was backed into a corner of the room and couldn't escape. I felt that this had happened many times. I filled the room with what I called the "Christ Light", and then went into each room and even the closets and did the same thing. When I went into the smaller of the two bedrooms, I got the feeling that something terrible had happened there that had caused great fear. When I finished, I told the apartment manager what I'd seen and felt. She said that a family that fit the description I gave her had moved out of that apartment just before her daughter had moved in. The man who had lived there with his family had beaten his wife and had molested his daughter in the small bedroom. I called the lady manager the next day to check on what was happening, and she said all was quiet. A couple of days later, she called to tell that it had started again. I remembered that she and my friend had stayed in the apartment with me and had been talking to one another constantly. When I went back there, I asked to be left alone in the apartment. I went through the same procedure as the first time and I was told later that there was not a recurrence of the troubling incidents or "hauntings". I decided that all the deep emotional trauma created in the apartment had left a "residue" that caused the manifestations. No ghost as such was involved.

Incidentally, this same apartment manager had a young son who would not go to school and she asked me if I could help with this problem. She said she had tried everything she could think of doing. He would start out to school but would come back home. I don't recall the exact method I used, but I got to the cause of his problem and worked that out. Then, I programmed him to want to go to school. I did all this while he was asleep at night and by "talking" to him mentally. Naturally, he was in his own home and I was in mine at the time. His mother said they no longer had a problem with this situation after that.

Another time, a friend asked me if I could find the cause of disturbances in her house, such as things falling down with no one in the room. I went to her house and saw an old man, in spirit form, standing in a doorway between two rooms. I asked him mentally what he was doing there and he said it was his home. He lived there and didn't want anyone else living there. I explained to him that he was dead and wasn't really living there, and that he needed to let go and move on. I asked my angel friends to help him and two of them came and led him "into the light". There were no more strange happenings.

One evening, my husband and I and another couple were invited to visit a friend of ours in another city. His wife had recently passed away. As we all sat talking, I saw a woman in spirit form at the top of some steps that led into another room. I told the man we were visiting what I was seeing and what she was wearing. He replied that his wife was dressed as I described her when she was buried. I carried on a mental conversation with her, and she wanted me to tell him she was well and happy. She wanted him to get on with his life and enjoy it. This seemed to help him to feel better.

I had a call one-day from a woman who had recently lost her husband in death. She was very distraught and thought I might help her to feel better. I went to her house and as we talked, I saw her husband's spirit and described him to her and she said it was, indeed, her husband. He pleaded with me to help her to understand that she needed to "let him go" and to tell her to find peace of mind or she would make herself very ill. I gave her this message and sent her healing thoughts in the days following. However, she continued to act as she had, and did actually have a "nervous breakdown".

I was playing bridge with friends one morning and as I glanced at my partner, I saw a sweet-faced old woman standing behind her. I described her to my partner, and she said it sounded like her grandmother's appearance. I mentally asked the old woman what she wanted. She said she wanted to wish her granddaughter a happy birthday. I asked her why she didn't wait until her granddaughter's birthday to do this, since I would be at the party. She replied that there would be too any people there and it would be difficult for me to see her. (It was a surprise party, so I couldn't tell my friend this part of the message at that time!) At the party, my friend showed me a photo of her grandmother, and it did look like the old woman I had seen in spirit form. I then told her the entire message I had received.

One of my oldest, dearest friends had lost her only son in an accident and I went to the funeral home to offer my condolences. I saw her son in spirit form trying to get his sister's attention, telling her "It's cool. Don't cry, I'm fine." and so on. He called her by name in a certain way that I was unfamiliar with. Since I didn't want to interrupt things, I decided to wait until after the burial to speak about this to my friend and her daughter. To my great surprise, as I drove to the cemetery I saw the young man sitting beside me. I asked him why he was in my car and not the one his mother and sister were in. He answered that they could neither see nor hear him. He wanted to be sure I'd tell them how happy he was, and for them to know he loved them. When I had an opportunity later to pass his message on, I repeated the name he had called his sister (I'd never heard him say it before) and his mother was very comforted, knowing it was a genuine message, because she said no one else called her daughter by that name.

I sometimes see discarnates when I go within and am doing cases. On day, I saw a friend who had passed away and she gave me a message for her family. They were very happy to receive this message, and found it helped them to feel better.

Almost all messages I get from discarnates are to let their loved one know that they are happy. I never call forth a spirit-I only make myself available if they choose to contact me and give me a message which I'm very happy to pass on to the person or persons for whom it was intended.

Many people wonder if animals have souls. There is something in them that survives death as many stories I have read indicate.

I have one of my own to relate.

Five of my friends and I were traveling in a large motor home. Some of us were seated opposite one another toward the back of it. As we talked, I saw a small black and white terrier-type dog come into that section and jump up on the seat opposite me and lie down next to one of the ladies. I knew it was a spirit form, because it was not quite solid. I asked the lady the dog had chosen to lie next to if she had such a pet. She replied that she had when she was a girl. Apparently, a strong bond had existed between them. I wonder how many times the little dog had been with her since it had passed on. I feel it is too bad she never knew her little pet was still with her at times.

# DEVILS, DEMONS AND HAUNTINGS

The following is a reading given to me in answer to questions I had about evil beings, how they got that way, how they function, and so on.

"There are no "devils" as such, only displaced souls who are "evil" in their thinking. They are "humans" in aspect, having a similar ancestry but unevolved humans who did not ascend the evolutionary path with their earth-oriented fellow beings. They are jealous of those on earth for having evolved to their present state, but cannot be born into a human body on their own volition, due to having made such a choice originally. (They, themselves, feel bound by this, but actually are not.) They are "wicked" because these attributes are given them by the human race because they terrify them. Originally, they did not manifest so. They would cause demonstrations of kinetic ability because they, being between worlds, did not lose the memory of how to accomplish these things. However, this caused fear in humans and caused the discarnates to be imprinted as "evil". They then began taking over bodies to further terrify people and gained much pleasure from this. They cannot, however, really take over anyone's soul, because the soul does not belong to the human being, but is part of God. God cannot allow part of God to be "damned" or "lost". These discarnates can actually be helped to begin the actual birth-death cycle here on earth and thus get out of the "in-between" world by helping them to realize they need not continue on their present course, that their decision need not be final, and that God does not hate them, but loves them, as God loves all that are part of Himself and all there is, are part of God. All the fear and thinking "evil" only reinforces and enlarges the "evil" which need not exist. Instead of exorcising these spirits and sending them back to whence their they came, it would stop their attacks and reduce their numbers if it were understood how to handle these things, and it was done by properly trained and highly evolved entities in human form.

As an added bit of information, there is primarily no difference between "devils" and "demons" except as there are in all life forms-some are leaders and some are followers and the energy fear amplifies can raise a "demon" to a "devil". Other than this, frightening experiences and demonstrations may be caused by discarnate souls between lives. They also need to be sent on by those who understand, because they too can be increasingly frightening as they are programmed and energized by wrong thinking-that is, fear.

Even those discarnates that are accepted as not harmful and are allowed to remain on the premises should be sent on their way. They are not pets!

Other manifestations can be caused by psychic energy building up, and even this can become frightening and harmful if it is not understood. It can lead to discarnates coming into the scene by attraction through fear.

"Possession" by discarnates cannot occur without some kind of invitation. God does not cause or permit this.

When fear has become so great, normal forms of prayer do not suffice, for they are imperfect at best for this purpose. As a rule, they denote fear more than faith. Prayers with power are those that affirm unity with God and God's power and knowing that our statements will be carried out. The prayers of exorcism are effective in the right person because they do align with God's power, but are only as effective as the person using them permits them to be. A feeling of love, sending light and an "understanding communication" would be far more effective in all cases.

Going "within" and uniting with God (or really becoming aware of this union) and feeling this overpowering love and holding this feeling while communicating with the discarnate, displaced soul, psychic energy, and so on would be the most beneficial because God is love, and love is the most powerful force there is.

# ON UFOs

At times, I was supposedly in communication with UFO occupants or aliens, as they are sometimes called. As I am basically a skeptic, I'd think, "Well, maybe."

During one of these meetings, I was told that to verify whether or not the communication was real, as proof, there would be several UFOs seen in our vicinity on a certain day. I duly reported this at the next meeting of the group I worked with, and it was recorded. The UFOs were actually seen there as promised, so I felt perhaps that I ought to accept my visits with the aliens as real.

Since I am discussing UFOs, I will mention a sighting that I experienced personally. This occurred at the time my family was living in a semi-rural community. My husband and I were in the den watching TV, and my fourth daughter and a friend were sitting in the back yard. It was about 9 PM. Suddenly; my daughter came in the house and asked me to join them outside. When I got out there, she pointed to a glow in the sky just above the treetops some distance away. She thought perhaps there was a big fire there or even that a plane had gone down. As we pondered the cause of the glow, it rose up into the air and began to come in our direction and to our right-south of us. We kept trying to figure out what it could be. At first, we thought it might be the Goodyear blimp, because as its side appeared at a distance, we could see what appeared to be windows, although we couldn't see anything else. All at once, it started coming directly toward us and then was soon in front of us. We could see three enormous lights all in a row, but there was no sound, even though it seemed almost directly above us within a stone's throw. We were still trying to decide what it was when the lights turned down towards us and we all instinctively jumped under trees. As we did this, it banked in a very sharp turn and went off to the north. As we watched, we saw a row of small colored lights, one white, then a red, then a white, a red, and another white. It got diminished in size very quickly and a haze seemed to envelop it. We finally heard a very muted motor sound. At no time did we see a fuselage or any type of body-only the different kinds of lights. I went into the house and called everyone I could think of that might have been able to tell us if there had been any kind of aircraft in the area at that time, but no one could account for it. As an added oddity to this event, when my daughter's friend tried to start her motorbike to go home, it wouldn't start. She told us later that when she got home, her bedroom light wouldn't turn on. My daughter's light in her bedroom didn't work either. But when I tried it, it came on.

I still don't know what we saw that night, nor could anyone else tell us, so I guess it qualifies as an Unidentified Flying Object!

As I was reading the book titled "Communion", I wondered if the beings described in it were in any way related to the ones I had been in contact with psychically. I was told the following: "In some cases they are from the "collective unconscious". You might say they are figments of the imagination. However, these are "real" figments and actually have a life of their own, assuming these identities to communicate with their "creators." THOUGHTS ARE THINGS AND HAVE SUBSTANCE! This substance can manifest in these forms and this is what had happened. However, as you were told there are real space beings. They too can communicate with you and sometimes do. Then, there are beings from other realms and dimensions who may choose to manifest in this way at times. They may also manifest on the mental planes to those who can communicate on that level as you can. Do not the "abductions" and "examination" seem pointless? And yet, there are physical evidences that they occur. This is a result of the human mind reaching out; desiring contact with those who may be further advanced. It is not always those who reach out who have these experiences".

At another time, I was told that some UFO occupants serve as liaisons between the physical and spiritual worlds, coming themselves from the mental realm. I was also told that these things sometimes happen to get our attention away from our earth-bound focus. They are letting us know that there are realities beyond our usual experience and to prepare us for the universal shift in consciousness, which will happen eventually.

# ON RELIGION

I make references in this book in several places about my Catholic upbringing.

Lest the reader should gather from some of my remarks that I disapprove of Catholicism, let me make my feelings clear on this and religion in general.

First of all, I do not regret being brought up on the Catholic faith. I was a devout and devoted Catholic for many years.

Also, I do not feel I've "fallen away" from the church. I do feel that I've "graduated" from the church and am grateful for all of the good things that I learned there. About angels for instance-all Catholic children are taught that they have guardian angels and to ask them for help and protection. This is just one of the many things I learned that have made my spiritual progress easier than it might have been. However, I have also had to "unlearn" many things. I had to learn to keep my mind open to instructions and information of all kinds on all levels and to know "my truth" when I found it-not to depend on what anyone else said I must believe.

I am not against any religion, provided it is not dogmatic and binding to the extent that people are not allowed to think for themselves under "pain of sin". All religions should help people to find God within themselves-not as some distant being far off in the clouds somewhere, and to know that God is a loving God-not angry and vindictive. This may have been God as seen by the ancients, but it is not God as Jesus knew Him and wants all to know Him.

By the same token, as I've said elsewhere in this book, I do not present anything as something you must believe. These are my truths and you must find and recognize what's true for you.

# HAPPENINGS

I have always been a very spiritual person, but at one time, I was also very religious. I attended mass faithfully every Sunday with my family.

After the birth of my fifth daughter, I tried taking her to church, but she was very active so I would stay in what we called "the crying room". That way, the rest of the congregation couldn't hear what as going on in there. The problem was that even with a loud speaker bringing the services into the room it was difficult to hear over the noise the little ones made.

I've always talked to God a lot and my faith has always been very strong. So I decided to ask God if it would be all right for me to stay at home with the baby on Sunday mornings. I also asked for a specific sign to let me know the answer. I love birds and always fed them on the patio. There seemed to be birds of all kinds feeding constantly. So I asked God to give me a sign. If it would be all right to stay at home, I asked that there would be no birds for an hour. There were no birds from that moment. At the end of the hour, they just flocked into the yard.

All of this occurred before I became involved in metaphysical studies and it really impresses upon me that God does indeed listen and answer us.

I needed help myself one day. At that time, we kept our horses out on the edge of town. After I took the children to school, I'd go out to feed the horses. On this particular morning, I drove back home and discovered that my house key was missing. It had been on the same ring as the car keys but must have fallen off somewhere in the pasture. I went within my mind and asked to see where the key was. I was shown a place outside the pasture fence near a certain post. I marked the location in my mind, returned to the pasture and went to the place I'd been shown. There was the key!

A different kind of "missing" case came up later. A woman called to ask if I could help her find her daughter. The girl had run away, and the mother was frantic. I went to my "special" mental place after I hung up the telephone. I saw the girl sitting on the steps of a beach house and talked to her mentally, telling her over and over to call her mother. The next day, the woman called me and said her daughter had called. She was at a house on the beach and her mother was very relieved to know that she was all right.

One day, I was on the way home from running errands when my car stopped in the middle of an intersection. It was a busy time of day and soon the air was filled with the sound of honking horns. Try as I would, the car just wouldn't start. So I decided to use healing energy on the car. I put my hands on the dashboard and sent the energy to wherever the problem might be. When I felt it was done (in a matter of a few minutes) I tried to start the car again and it started right away. It gave me no further trouble all the way home and into the driveway. When my husband came home, I told him what had happened. He went out to see what could have caused the problem. When he came in, he looked at me and said that there was no way that car could be driven, as a wire was completely separated. I just looked at him and smiled because there had been a way!

There was a day when I thought I had learned all that I needed to learn, metaphysically speaking. I decided that now I could sit back and put my life in God's hands and make no more effort to struggle, to cope, and to learn. However, I was brought up short when a voice within me said, "If this is all there is, why have you learned all that you have?"

Then, I was shown a very small child walking along between her parents, holding their hands and feeling so loved and protected. She was totally dependent on them with not a worry in the world. I was made to understand that loving parents expected their child to learn as it grew until it didn't need their constant supervision. The child was expected to become a mature adult capable of leading it's own life. I understood that as far as my spiritual progress was concerned, I was thinking like that little child. If I expected to reach my fullest spiritual growth I must continue to learn, seek, and find answers. God and my angels would always be there to help, but I must go on doing my part. As the years have gone by, I now understand that the more I learn, the more I realize how very much more there is to learn.

I went to California to visit my oldest daughter. While I was there, she took me to visit the University of California Neuropsychological Institute where I met with Dr. John Hubacher. He decided to test my abilities. He conducted experiments at the institute while I was back at my daughter's house. He told me that he was going to go outside and pick two leaves and punch holes in them. I was to then send healing energy to the leaves. When he called me I told him he had punched a hole in one, but had slit the other. He told me that I was correct, that he had done it to test me. He took pictures, using Kirlian photography before and after I sent healing energy to the leaves. The "after" photo showed a large cloud of energy around the leaves. The "before" photo just had an outline around the leaves. He wanted to perform more tests, but I had to get back home. It was near Christmas, and I had my little ones to think about. I thoroughly enjoyed the testing and wished I'd had more time.

We had moved out of the city so that we could keep our horses on our own property.

At the time I will now tell about, we had three horses in the corral. They would often get out somehow and our neighbors would call us to let us know. We would then have to round them up and bring them back.

We were awakened one night by one of our neighbors calling to tell us that the horses were out again. The girls, their dad and I went out to look for them. The first two were quickly found, and we put them in the stable, but the third one wanted to play. It would wait until we got close and then run off again. I finally decided to try using my mind to get it home. I stood still, closed my eyes and "went within". I imagined I was the horse. I said, "What am I doing out here all alone? My friends are in the stable. I don't like it out here anymore". I kept this up for a few minutes and suddenly the horse just turned around and trotted through the gate which the girls were holding open and went right into the stable all by itself. I thought to myself, "What a wonderful gift God has given us-this mind with which we can contact others in a beneficial way."

As many of you already know, if you are a student or practitioner of metaphysics it is possible to actually project one's awareness anywhere and be there mentally with all senses functioning. I personally do not do this often except when necessary, as when doing cases, but one time I did it deliberately. My parents had moved into a new residence in another state. I wanted to visit them but couldn't get away at that time, so I determined to visit them mentally. I visualized myself going towards their new home. I found myself outside their door and went in, going through each room and looking at everything. Later, when I had the opportunity to visit them in person, I found everything much as I had "seen" it during my mental visit. However, when I went into the kitchen, I noticed that the refrigerator was a different color than I had "seen" it to be. I felt disappointed because I thought my "mind" trip had been faulty. I told my mother that I had thought the refrigerator was green but the one I saw here was pink. She smiled and told me that they had a green one at that time, but it had stopped working and they had replaced it with the pink one!

I had been experimenting with weather control, primarily at stopping rain. We'd been having an overabundance in our area. I found that it usually took about five minutes to stop an average rainfall, a bit longer for a heavy one. I put this to good use on rainy days when my children rode the school bus home. Our driveway was very long and they were let out at the road. If it was raining, they could be soaked by the time they reached the house. About five minutes or so before the bus was due, I'd start using my mind to cause the rain to stop. I visualized them getting into the house without getting wet. This would always happen and it usually started raining again as soon as they got inside the house. I still use this technique when I'm out running errands or leaving somewhere and it's raining. If I have an umbrella, I don't do this if we need rain.

Recounting this reminds me of a time that my children and some of the neighborhood children were planning a little affair on our property. They had planned games, contests, pony rides, and so on. As the time drew near on the day it was scheduled, the sky became overcast. My children cam in to ask me, "Please don't let it rain!" As soon as they went back outside, I started visualizing a big canopy over our property, which consisted of about three acres. There were roads on all four sides of it. (I visualized angels holding the canopy up!) It started raining very hard all around our property, but only a few drops fell on our grounds. The children all had a good time, but it rained so hard all around that some areas were flooded.

One bright, sunny morning, I hurried through my housework because I had several cases to work on. I went into my bedroom and closed the draperies to darken the room. I sat against the headboard of my bed to do my cases. I was meditating and praying as I always did before doing this work. Suddenly, there was the sound of a terrific explosion right next to the bed. I was startled and opened my eyes to see what had happened. All was as usual! I read later, somewhere that such a thing sometimes happens when a person arrives at a new level spiritually. It had sounded just like a transformer blowing - first a buzzing sound, and then a tremendously loud bang.

Another day, I was again in my darkened room doing cases when I felt a strong light against my closed eyes. I thought perhaps the drapes had come apart and let the sunlight in. When I opened my eyes, the room was still dark, but there were little specks of light, dancing about like fireflies throughout the room. It was a wonderful sight and I repeatedly shut my eyes and opened them again to enjoy this delightful spectacle. Finally, it stopped and I resumed doing my cases filled with a sense of wonder. It never happened again, although I wanted it to so very much. It was later explained to me by my inner wisdom that this had been a manifestation of enlightenment, the first step!

I was at a club with friends one night wearing long, dangly beaded earrings. Early in the evening, I had admired them in the mirror in the powder room. Later, when I went back in there, looking in the mirror I noticed one was missing. We looked everywhere for it, including on the floor. We used a flashlight, but could not find it. I hated losing it because it was part of a set with a matching necklace. We finally decided to leave and went out to the car. When we opened the door, I found the earring on the front seat on the driver's side. Since I was the first one in the car, I knew none of us had put it there. I knew my angel had been at work.

Working at the kitchen sink one night after dinner, I took off my watch and put it on the cabinet top behind me. I was alone in the house. The children were all playing outside. I finished my task and turned around to pick up my watch and put it on. It was gone. I looked on the floor and all around, but, since I had put it on the middle of the counter, I didn't expect to find it any other place. I really missed the watch because I'd had it for several years and had a sentimental attachment to it. Several weeks later, I decided to give my closet a thorough cleaning and took everything off the floor. There, back in a corner, I saw my watch and another piece of jewelry that had been missing. How did they get there? Playful spirits? At any rate, I informed whoever was responsible that I didn't appreciate that kind of joke. I suggested that they should put their talents to better use. Later, I finally replaced that watch with another one, but I kept the old one and put it in my jewelry chest. For a long time, whenever I looked at it, the time was always correct even though I hadn't wound it for months.

This reminds me of another watch story. I had given my father a self-winding watch in the days before quartz movements. He had it a long time and while I was visiting one day, he told me it no longer worked. I took it and held it in my hands while we visited and then put it to my ear. It was ticking merrily along and continued to work without further trouble for a long time.

I was alone in the house one day getting ready to do the dishes. I was at the sink and, looking outside, I noticed it was getting very dark. A storm was threatening. I had my hands in the water and turned away from the sink to pick up something behind me. Suddenly, there was a loud blast and the entire kitchen was lit by a blinding light. As I turned back to the sink, I saw that a pile of stainless steel flatware was welded into one piece! It had been lying on the rim of the stainless steel sink. We found later that one of our trees close to the house had been hit by lightening. The bolt had traveled down the tree, along the water lines and into the house. Had I not turned away from the sink, I would surely have been hit. This may not seem to have any psychic connection, but why did I turn away from the sink just before the lightning hit? I feel I was being protected. My time had not come.

As I was dropping off to sleep one night, my vanity lamp came on by itself. I went to my dressing table and turned it off. I thought it was odd because it was very hard to turn on and off.

Later that same night, I was awakened by a loud thump. I turned on the bedside lamp and found my purse upside down on the floor. It was wide open, but nothing had spilled out. When I picked it up, everything fell out! I couldn't understand how it could have fallen. I had put it on a console against the wall in the opposite position of the edge. It had actually landed two or three feet away from the edge. I pondered over this for a few minutes, and then went back to bed.

The next morning as I ate my breakfast and read the paper, my chair started vibrating. Finally, it was loud enough to hear it clattering on the floor.

Then I knew that these episodes were the forerunner of some special thing about to happen. I had no idea of what it might be. I put it out of my mind because I had a busy day ahead of me.

That night, my husband and I went to visit another couple for a game of bridge. As we sat talking before starting the game, a voice within me said, "Look at your hands." I looked at the backs of my hands and saw nothing out of the ordinary. Then I was told, "Look at you palms." I did so and much to my surprise saw an indentation in the middle of each palm. Then I knew this represented the healing done through me. The depressions were where so many pictures show the wounds in Jesus' hands where the nails had been driven. I knew the marks in my palms were symbolic because I think the nails that held Jesus' arms to the cross were driven into his wrists below his hands.

I deeply appreciated this manifestation, although I had never expected anything like this to happen.

One evening as I was putting silverware into the dishwasher, I was reminded of the spoon bending feats of the psychic Uri Geller. I thought to myself that I'd rather straighten things out that were bent. Later, when I took the silverware out to put it away, one of the forks was perfectly straight. It looked as if a steamroller had run over it!

Many years later, one of my daughters and I were talking of this on the phone. After we hung up, she picked up her key ring to go out. She was shocked to see two of her keys were bent. She had to use pliers to get them straight enough to use them.

A neighbor I had never met called me one day and said she had heard that I could help people with problems. She asked me if I could find out what happened to a very expensive ring her husband had given to her recently. She didn't know if it had slipped off her finger into some trash she had taken out that had been picked up. She was desperate and didn't want to tell her husband that she couldn't find it. I told her I'd do what I could. I went to my inner mind and saw her ring in a corner of the bathroom vanity behind a can of hairspray. When I called her back to tell her this, she said it couldn't be there. She had taken everything off that vanity top while searching for her ring and it hadn't been there. I told her I'd hold the phone while she looked there again. She came back in a short time and told me it had been exactly where I had seen it. She was absolutely amazed. How did it get there? I never questioned how. I just knew it was there.

Another incident involving a ring took place in my hometown. I had come from another state to visit my family. I visited my parents in their home for a few days and then took my mother to visit my sister in another city. When it was time to take my mom back home, she became very upset. She couldn't find a ring I had given her for Mother's Day. It was gold and had a gold rose on it because she loved roses. Using my mind, I didn't see the ring anywhere, but I was told, "Tell her not worry. She will get it back." We drove to her house and she went into her bedroom to start unpacking and came out immediately. She was holding her ring, her face was pale, and she said, "It was on top of my chest of drawers. It looked huge and there was a light all around it!"

I was preparing to go out one afternoon and was seated on the side of the bed putting on my stockings when something plopped onto the floor in front of me. I picked up a little gold flower in the shape of a lily. I looked up on the ceiling, but there was nothing up there it could have come from. I still have it after many years and treasure it as a gift from beyond.

Just recently, I noticed the little clock on the bathroom vanity top was 15 minutes slow. Apparently, it needed a new battery. I took it to the kitchen and removed the old battery and then did another chore. When I finally put a new battery in the clock, I turned the clock over and was surprised to see the time was accurate. Somehow, without my moving the clock's hands, it had made up the time that it had lost!

# WALK-INS

I will now discuss something, which may be the most controversial topic in this book.

If you have read widely on metaphysical subjects, you may be familiar with the term "walk-ins". If you have heard of it and accept it as a possibility, you may also believe that this cannot occur more than once in a body's lifetime.

I am going to relate what happened in and to this body in which I dwell. You are certainly free to accept it or not. It is my truth.

First, let me explain my description of a "walk-in". One entity, or soul, leaves the body and another comes in so the body does not die. This is not "possession" such as an entity just taking over a body in spite of the occupying soul. Walk-ins occur with the permission of the departing soul who has finished its current cycle here on earth. It willingly leaves the body to allow it to be used by another soul. The entering soul can then accomplish whatever it needs to in earthly learning and experience without going through a whole life cycle. This is done in cooperation with the Oversoul of the body who is in charge of many souls.

I, the present soul, have the memories of the lives of all the souls who have dwelled for a time in this body. This is possible because all of these memories are stored in this brain which we all have shared. This helps each soul to continue the life of this body without too many traumas.

Most walk-ins may not realize that they are indeed walk-ins!

I will tell the story of each soul who was a tenant for a time in this body and use the first person. This will make it easier to follow.

The first soul was born into this body and lived in it for over forty years. This is her story.

I had been ill for several days, but did my best to just keep going. I hadn't gone to a doctor because I kept thinking I'd feel better the next day. On that weekend, my husband was at home so I just stayed in bed. Finally, in spite of feeling very weak and tired, I decided to get up anyhow. I changed the bed, took a bath, and put on a fresh gown, robe, and slippers. I then slowly made my way to the den to see how my family was getting along. They were doing all right, so I went back to bed. As I lay there, I began to hear the most beautiful singing I had ever heard. I had my eyes closed enjoying this singing when the room suddenly seemed to darken. I thought perhaps a storm was coming, but when I opened my eyes, the sun was shining brightly. As soon as I opened my eyes, the singing stopped. This happened several times. Then, while my eyes were open, the room began to get darker and smaller. Finally, it seemed to come completely together-ceiling, walls, and floor. I fell into a deep sleep. This is when I left the body and walk-in Number One came in.

**Walk-in Number One**

I didn't know I was new to my body. I just felt there had been a change in me. I started thinking differently about things. I became deeply interested in psychic phenomena, metaphysical subjects, and healing, in particular. I read everything I could on these subjects and would walk around with a book in my hand while doing housework. I even read at the table during meals and into the night.

The section of this book titled "Introduction" tells this part of my story, but I must expand on it.

I had been reading about healing with the hands and I felt that I could do this. At the time, our pet guinea pig gave birth to three babies-one for each of my daughters. They seemed to be doing fine until one morning we noticed that one of them was dragging its hind legs. Its eyes were cloudy. By night, it was dead. We all felt terrible about it. To our dismay, the next morning another baby was showing the same symptoms. I decided to pray for it. I picked it up, held it in my hands, and asked God to please heal it. I felt a tingling like electricity in my arms and hands. I continued to hold it and pray and then put it back in the cage. Imagine our delight to see it soon begin running about as if nothing had been wrong with it! Now I knew I could be an instrument for healing.

A few days later, my youngest child got up in the morning with a fever and threw up her breakfast. I told her to lie down on the sofa and put my hands on her stomach and prayed for her healing and again felt the tingling in my hands and arms. In a few minutes, she sat up and said she wanted to eat breakfast again! I felt so elated knowing that God was healing through me!

Then I began wondering about all the other things I had read about. I felt I could do some of these things too if I just could find the "key". I continued to read, study, practice, and experiment. I found I could actually do many of the things I had read about.

In the meantime, I was becoming more and more discontented with my appearance. Looking into a mirror, I saw dark hair but I "knew" I was supposed to be a blond! Finally, I did become a blond and then felt like "myself".

During these years I had made many new friends due to my metaphysical activities. Some of them were fellow students. Others were acquainted through coming to me for help of one kind or another. Among these friends was a young man who was both a client and a student of metaphysics. You might say I served as his "guru" or teacher.

A past life reading for him showed that we had been together in various roles in past lives. I tell this particular story because it is unusual.

Feeling extremely tired one afternoon, I decided to take a nap. As I lay there, I immediately went into a state of altered consciousness. I "saw" myself lying down on a sort of gurney. I saw my friend's body suspended over mine and then come down, his back facing me, and merge with my body. I both heard and saw the words; "this is a bonding". Then I was told to call him and tell him what had just happened. I felt so terribly tired that I said I'd do it when I woke up. I was told, "Do it now!" I was barely able to dial his number because I felt so weak and exhausted, but I did as was told. My voice was barely audible as I related to him what had happened. Then, without conscious thought, I said, "I suppose now you'll have sinus problems." (I had severe sinus problems at times.) He replied that wouldn't happen-he never had any sinus problems. I hung up the phone and fell into a deep sleep. I left the body and Walk-in Number Two came in.

## Walk-in Number Two

I had known beforehand that I would be the next occupant of this body. I was so eager to be in it that on a few occasions I had attempted to come in so I could familiarize myself with being in a human body. Being from the mental realm, I had never had a physical body before.

At these times, Number One, who was ordinarily rather lithe and graceful became clumsy and awkward. It was like two people trying to drive a car at the same time. She would drop and spill things and bump into furniture. She would wonder what in the word was the matter with her.

The day after I "came in", I went to see the young man mentioned earlier. I couldn't help being amused to find he had a bad sinus headache. He was also holding his right hand with a "limp" wrist. This was one of Number One's traits.

I told him Number One was gone. He was shocked and saddened, but I was elated. I'd had no experience with human relations and emotions. I had come to do a job, but I was going to have fun doing it!

It was necessary for me to behave in general as if I was still Number One, but I felt rather immune to the ups and downs of human "feelings". As time went by, I gradually grew more sympathetic, but not entirely.

However, every time I saw myself in the mirror, I didn't like the blond hair. I had decided before I came into this body that I would have red hair. When I finally dyed my hair red, I felt like "myself".

Actually, my main purpose in "coming in" was to get a divorce. Number One had been too kind to do this, but I didn't have any second thoughts. Even before the divorce was final, I had moved to another city. There I studied metaphysics, did counseling (metaphysical), and made many new friends.

After a while, I decided to go to work in the apartment business and worked in this field for several years. I really enjoyed that work, but kept on with metaphysical studies and related activities. I found being in a human body interesting, challenging, and fun.

For some reason, I began to feel that I should give my former marriage another chance. The thought of this really depressed me. However, my former husband agreed that we should do it. We were married quickly and quietly in spite of the fact that he had been dating another woman. I didn't like this remarriage and wondered why on earth I had done it.

To complicate matters, I had just taken a new position as manager of an apartment complex and was about to move. I moved into my new apartment and I was trying to adjust to being married again, a new home and a new job.

The marriage was not working for either of us and we agreed to have it annulled. In a very short time, my former husband and his lady friend were married. I felt very relieved. Now he wouldn't be lonely and I could get on with my life. Our remarriage had been for him and I felt good about that.

Several months went by and then my life in this body came to an end. As I was falling asleep one night, Mother/Father God came to me and took my hands in theirs. We went to a place on the inner planes. We stood on a white platform with a white arch over it. All around us was black nothingness. I was told to "jump off". Without hesitation, I did so and at this time, Number Three came into the body.

**Walk-In Number Three**

I awoke in the morning feeling disoriented. I felt very confused, but I had to present an appearance of a calm, poised person for my work. I was managing an apartment complex and had a great deal of responsibility.

Gradually, I began to feel more comfortable, but still couldn't figure out why I had felt so unsettled for a while. Like Number One, I did not realize that I was a walk-in.

My life in this body was rather uneventful except for one thing. I was in an altered state of consciousness one day when I was shown the face of a man. I was told that this was my next husband. I remember thinking that I hadn't planned on marrying again. In fact, I was planning to retire and move to Mexico in six months. I had visited Guadalajara several years before and loved it. I expected to live very simply and work with the poor people there, helping and healing. As I was thinking about all this, I was shown a speeding freight train and given to understand that this was symbolic, showing me how forcefully this man would come into my life and couldn't be stopped.

A few months later, I actually did meet this man. Ten days after we met, he asked me to marry him. I accepted with joy because I knew we were meant to be together. We were married a month later. I moved into his house and started an entirely different life-style. I was, again, a homemaker. We got a dog, I made new friends, and became a suburbanite.

People still called me for help with their various problems, but, except for my family, I did no healing in person. I still meditated daily and continued to find peace and inner strength through this practice. I kept in contact with my dear ones on the inner planes. Basically, however, my life was that of a typical wife and homemaker.

Very few people knew the "real" me, the metaphysician become mystic. I felt my life was "on hold". This, in fact, was true. I was literally keeping this body alive for the next occupant, but of course, I didn't know that at the time. I just knew I was where I was supposed to be and tried to be contented. I kept on meditating and doing healing and helping, but only a few of my new friends knew I did these things. Gradually, I let more people know, but my mystical side was never fully revealed. I kept busy enough helping others who knew what I did, became very ill, and it took about three months to recover and during that time, I left the body. My leaving was uneventful, quiet, and beautiful. Mother/Father God escorted me to the inner realms and the present soul came in.

## Walk-in Number Four

I am told that I am a new soul-that I have never existed before. I was puzzled because I wondered why I had been put in an aging body. Why wasn't I born as a baby and allowed to grow up like others? I was told that it was to give me a "head start" on my next life.

To help me to understand, I was given readings at various times. These were literally dictated to me and I wrote them down as they were being told to me. They have helped me to understand many things and I am most grateful.

I have many times felt that I am not living up to my potential. At these times, I ask for a reading and they are a big help to me. They reassure me and help me to be patient.

One of the things I've been given to do is to write this book. It may be that it will be my last work on this earth plane in this body. If that is so, I am ready to leave whenever it is my time. I am already looking forward to my next time on earth. What I have been told about that is revealed in the readings that follow. They are numbered according to the number of the entity in the body at the time they were given.

# MEETING MEGA

Some months ago, I spent several days at the lovely home of friends who lived in the Texas hill country.

One day they had gone out to run several errands and I chose to stay alone so I could meditate. As soon as I reached a meditative level I saw a powerfully built, enormous female form. She was dressed as a warrior-woman. She wore a knee-length tunic, girded at the waist. Her stockings were a heavy material and she had on open-front boots that laced up to her knees. Her dark blond hair hung in two heavy braids over her shoulders and she carried a long spear. As I watched her I noticed, closer to me, a very beautiful female form. She wore flowing robes of a soft old-rose color and the folds deepened from lavender to purple. While her face was beautiful, it was not what I'd call pretty, but strong in a classical Greek sort of way. An aura of utter peace and love flowed from her. I asked her who she was, and she replied "True Self". When I asked her where she had come from, she replied, "I have always been here." I thought I was meeting my guardian angel and seeing her in two different aspects. As time went on, I began to feel this was not quite correct. I was eventually given to understand that she is my "over soul" as well as the over-soul of all the souls who have been occupants of this body. The warrior woman is indeed my guardian angel, but is also an extension of my over-soul.

Later, as I greeted my over-soul, I kept seeing the word "Mega" in front of her. I finally asked in what context it was used and I was told to "look it up." So I looked in my largest dictionary and found, as I knew, it meant "Great, Mighty, Powerful." This fits very well my feelings about her. This is her name and she said it is pronounced "Meega". I asked her why it had taken so long to meet her, and was told that she wanted the others to experience earthly life through this body, but now that phase was over.

For quite a while, as I saw her, she seemed to come partly into my body at times. I asked her about this and she said the vibrations still weren't at a level where she would be comfortable if she came in completely. I still had work to do, spiritual work.

Finally, very recently, she has been able to come in completely. Now she comes in at times to help raise my vibrations. This is not like a walk-in or soul possession as I am part of her.

Now I am working on realizing all that this means. I do understand that I wasn't ready to start writing this book until I met her and I've asked her to write it through me. I feel she is doing this, but expressing in my own words.

I have also come to understand her true nature as I've become better acquainted with her. She is one of the "faithful" angels who did not rebel against God. She has been helping souls to find their way back to their original state since the beginning.

As I have gained spiritual knowledge with her help, I put less emphasis on what I can do psychically and spend more time developing my own spirituality. For a long time I was uncomfortable with this, feeling that I should devote my time and efforts to sending help to those in need. Now I remember that these things are side-effects of spiritual progress and we must make that our goal. Not that I think it's all right to ignore opportunities to help others. I still do these things, but I no longer feel the dedication to them that I once did. They are not the reason for my existence. The true purpose of my life is realizing oneness with God and I do feel this at times, more and more often, but I want this feeling of oneness to be constant. This is my goal, and Mega will be with me, all the way, on this journey.

# COMMUNICATIONS
# READINGS FOR NUMBER ONE

One night as I was falling asleep, I was told that this was my last night on earth. I thought this meant that I would die during the night. This was all right with me, and I asked if this was so, but I received no answer. A little later as I was again falling asleep, I was told that when I awoke I would be the Christ of me. I was elated, thinking that when I awoke in the morning I would truly be the Christ of me. I was disappointed when I got up and was still the same as when I went to bed.

After meditating on the meaning of these messages, I realized that I was being told that I was in the last "night" or "darkness" on this earth. When I would awake to the full realization as to whom or what I really was, I would then know that I was the "Christ" of me. Out of the darkness into the light of realization of oneness with God!

Reading for Number One from Mother/Father God

This was given to me while I still married to the first husband.

"All is "on hold" until you leave. You can accomplish nothing in your present situation. You are wasting our time. Think not of your home. Home is where you are, not a house. You need to be free, to express the "real you" that you are. The time with the family is over. They do not need you as much as you believe.

"You are concerned with financial loss. You will not lose with Me. I will guide and protect you always and bring all good to you.

"Believe in Me, beloved child and let Me express My bounty through you."

She then named the city I was to move to and said, "That is your new place. There you will find all you need for fulfillment-all will fall into place. Some must stay in a place to experience what they need. You must leave to experience what you want. You have no karma here except what you claim! It is not yours-you borrowed the body, not the penalties!

"You have all the power you need and want if you will release it. You cannot do this if you remain in the mold of the old identity. It confines and constrains you and it is not yours! I will see to the children." (They were no longer small.) I will bless you if you do as I say, but I cannot help you if you stay.

"You are not doing what you came to do. Being here has a bad influence on you and you are becoming negative and confused. Embark on this project and I will bless you.

"Possessions do not possess you, but you need something to start out with. (Here I was told what to take with me.) I will find lucrative employment for you in (The name of the city was given.) This will permit you the freedom to do as you desire and as I desire you to do. The environment there is conducive to bringing out the best in you. You will fell better and look better and accomplish what you came to do. Now, do it!"

The following reading was given to Walk-in Number Three:

"We are delighted that you have taken up the pen again to record our conversations. There is much to relate of other times and people. Some of it will be new to you and some of it you already know.

"There was a time when you did not exist in this body, as you know. At that time, you were with us gaining much information and insight, which we wish to be shared with humanity.

"To start: when you came back her after the last time in a body you were not quite 'finished', so to speak. You needed additional 'refining' and 'refinishing'.

"While you were here, the one called Number Two came into the body and manifested in a unique way. We will not go into detail, but will clarify her mission. Besides getting the divorce, it was, as you surmised, a "grounding" for other beings from that realm to enable them to communicate and interact with humanity. This will raise the genetic vibrations to enable the next wave of consciousness to manifest (those of us from the realm of spirit) and this was done. Then you came in and performed the same function for those in the spiritual realm to enable them to communicate and interact with humanity. The vibrations were proper for you to reenter with your new concepts and information. You understand that none of this is unique, as the same thing has transpired all over the world. There are always those who volunteer to do this on these planes.

"It is true that you were originally from the angelic realm and 'fell' because of self-pride. You discounted the source of your power and gifts, thinking they originated in you-the original sin! You were cast out down onto earth to begin your sojourn back to us. This all occurred many millenniums ago. At this time, we will not go into all the phases and life-forms that you have endured on this earth which was indeed your 'hell', your place of learning.

"Slowly, slowly you were permitted to remember bits and pieces of your true nature, ever striving to recapture the feeling of utter bliss and fulfillment that was your natural state before you 'fell'. Myriad others were of your company-some were leaders, most were followers, all in error. The real 'hell' was in flashes of knowledge of your former state and knowing how far from it you were at various times.

"Thus again I say, slowly, slowly you came into realization on both levels of your true state of being. Now you are returned to us on this level (in altered states of consciousness). While still functioning on that level. We are using you now, at your insistence, to help others of your ilk to realize more quickly who and what they really are. Therefore, we have decided to bestow on you there some of the miracles you can do here (on the inner planes) using your mind and the power.

"Now you know it's true source and never again will you forget! Keep humble and know your true happiness is in serving as an expression of the God energy that it may express and experience through you.

"Such love fills you now and this makes our task easy, for love is the energy form that is most easily transmuted into expression of various ways of helping humanity. This will you fellow creatures come to know their own potential."

At a later date:

One night I could not sleep for a long time and began meditating and communicating and was given information, which elated me. The next morning I said to myself, "I hope I can remember it and write it down as I understand it." The message was for me, but I know it was also for all that are earnestly seeking to be as spiritually perfect as possible. We do not do this out of vanity or self-pride, but because we love God and want to serve as perfectly as possible.

I was told we already have everything we need and want without having to ask for it. This is because before we are even aware of wanting or needing it, God knows and it is there! We need only to claim it and accept it, not from God but from ourselves since we are the ones keeping it from ourselves. Our mortal minds have been programmed to expect lack instead of fulfillment!

We already have all the precious qualities we have prayed for if we would only realize it. God made us in His own image and likeness and God is perfect. We have hidden our perfection from ourselves. (Due to "guilt", "unworthiness", etc.?). All that God has is ours. We need only to realize it, to understand that this is so. We may know it, but unless we understand it, we are bound by our feelings of limitation.

We need not feel greedy in expecting all that is good and desirable for body, mind and soul. Our Mother/Father God yearns to give us all we desire (that is good for us) just as mortal parents desire to give their children what they want if it is good for them.

Of course, we must dedicate our lives to God, make God a "senior partner" in this enterprise. It is also important to accept "Divine Love, Wisdom, Knowledge and Power" as our birthright and work with and for God, not only when we receive any good in our live, but even before we receive it, because it is there for us.

# COMMUNICATION
## (For Entity before Mega)

At times I get "feelings" about things that occur in my life or the lives of other people and I ask about them when I meditate. Often, I am told to write it down as it is being given to me which I do like taking dictation.

I have been told, at one time, that I was a new soul. I wondered why I was not put in infant body and allowed to grow up in a normal way. Why was I put in this mature body?

I wanted to know the reason for my existence at this particular time. (I had my own ideas on this!)

The reading that follows was given to me by my female God-aspect:

"You are correct. Your reason for being on earth is to become accustomed to being in a human body, to know how illness feels, how difficult relationships can be, how frustrating defeats and lacks can be. It is all part of the human condition. As a new soul without this experience and without these memories of those in this body before you, it would be too difficult to function as you must when you come back to do your real work in your next life.

"As you concluded last night, it (my next life) is to propagandize the dual nature of God-both male and female-each utterly equal in their functions.

"It is not necessary that you concentrate on healing and other spiritual and metaphysical aspects of your nature at this time. They will come to the fore in your next lifetime so that you will be able to convince people of your authenticity as My spokesperson.

"Do keep up what you are doing-going to level and communicating (most important!) and healing and so on, but these are just aids to your real work, not goals in themselves."

Another communication from Mother/God:

"Today we speak of origins. As you know, you are a new soul created by us for an express purpose-to help people learn and understand that God is equally male and female and has always been.

"At one time, all adored a female God and other times a male God. Now it is time that all understand God's dual being. One God-two natures. One incomplete without the other. One creative (female) and one to carry out the creation (male).

"Of course, this is extremely simplified, but in essence it is so. Until all humanity understands this, there can be no true peace or evolvement."

Communication the following day from Mother/God:

"It is true your subconscious plays a part in these messages but only as an instrument for Us to communicate through. At times, there may seem to be a distortion as per the first and last of this series to date, but be not apprehensive-all is true.

"We are very concerned that your life be truly fulfilling and happy and prosperous, but it needn't be if you'd rather not! (I could think negatively and of lack.) Let it happen! Do not worry as if you are a dog with a bone. Take one day at a time and do the best you can."

In spite of all I was told, at times I still continue to be too concerned about things. The following reading relates to this-

"My dear one, you are disturbed because your mind/body/brain/metaphysical abilities do not seem to be what you feel they should be. Do not be dismayed because this is a period of respite, of resting, if you will. There is much going on in the inner planes that has to do with these things. We are actually working on all these things.

"When your car is taken in for a "tune-up" can you drive it? Under the circumstances, you are doing well. Just "coast" along and do the best you can. You will find an improvement in these things shortly. Your life is about to change and you will have other things to focus on. They will take your attention. After that the changes you desire (improvements) will be obvious. You have much groundwork to do in this lifetime, so your next life will have a head start. The rest of your life will be interesting and fun.

"In fact, though your next lifetime will be devoted to "The Work", even so you will enjoy it. Do not fret-all is well."


Again, a short time later I was given another message because I still felt I was not functioning as I should. How patient God is with me!

"You feel frustrated and inept-like you're not living up to your potential-that your life needs 'perking' up.

"Be not sad about your life. It is good and you do well. However, we understand that you'd like some happy excitement to liven things up, so be prepared. All "Heaven" is about to burst forth. It will energize you and make you feel glad to be alive. We won't tell you exactly what will happen or when, but be prepared and expect your life to change for the better. We're talking about the way you feel about yourself, not your life as it actually is, because it is already good!"

I had been accustomed to living a more interesting life than I was experiencing at the above time. However, I realize, in looking back, that I have experienced so much fulfillment in my life because of my own attitude. I don't mean to say that I was discontented, but I felt a lack of fulfillment, which, as I say, I kept from myself! Again, I had to be "consoled"-

A few weeks later...

"Dear one, you are feeling tired and depressed again. I understand you feel you have no reason to feel so and indeed consider yourself fortunate compared to so many others. Aren't you aware that frustration can make you feel so? You are waiting for something to happen that you have been told will happen. And you are tired of waiting! This is normal. Be assured that all will happen as promised when it is time! Would you take a cake out of the oven before it was done? Be not impatient-it will happen soon enough-"

In reading this again, I am so impressed with the infinite love and patience God has toward me. I know that I do not have even the vaguest thought that God is not aware of. I know we are one. These days, I am practicing feeling and realizing that union every time I think of it, which is increasingly often.

I must add here that, overall; no one is more special in God's mind than any other person. However, we are very special to that part of God that dwells in each of us. Not only are we special; we are the "only child" of that part of God.

The following discourse is between God and me in September 1991:

Me: "Dear Ones, I am confused as to my role in our relationship. Am I to put myself at Your complete disposal and be an extension of You on the earth? Or am I to be an individual, to go forth using the gifts You have given me as the need occurs, but still working with You and my angels? One time, I think the first and then the latter. Will you please enlighten me?"

God: "Will you work with Me as an extension of Myself like a child who is grown goes into business with it's parents? Will you let Me guide you as a loving parent who is preparing it's child to take over the family business? In other words, there is a middle course in which we communicate and help one another for the common good. You are part of Me, it's true, but with your own identity and must express yourself too. We are like-minded, so if you are in doubt about anything in particular, just ask. If you want Our help, just ask. We are all here to help you. Your angels are like nurses in an operating room and you are the doctor. They all have their specific duties and know them so you needn't ask them. They stand by ready to help you go along like a well-trained team."

Again, in October 1991, I felt I needed to better understand these things so again I asked.

Me: "I am confused as to what my attitude should be. Am I to ask You for help in doing cases, etc.? Or should I realize that You have given me Your power to direct where and how I will?

I always do cases with the understanding that if it is not according to divine plan it will not happen."

God: ""If We want to intercede We will without your asking. You have Our permission to use the power as you will-it is Our gift to you. Be confident as a mature practitioner should be. Know that Our will is one. Have I not told you so?"

Me: "But what if it is someone's time to die and I send healing or protection so they will not."

God: "Then they will die if it is indeed their time. Often it can be that there is a choice for that soul to go on here and they may accept that if the help is forthcoming."

Me: "But what if they need an experience or illness or whatever as a learning experience?"

God: "You can help them to learn through grace. Also, it may be that they have learned but, because of habit or wrong thinking, cling to their problem. You can help by breaking the cycle and helping them to understand so they don't need the experience any longer. The "power" is intelligent and will assist in whatever manner is most effective.

"But don't forget, all have freedom of choice. While wanting and accepting help with the conscious mind, their subconscious can reject it for any number of reasons. Remember, as you so often have said, you don't take the responsibility for healing, or the credit! The power is Mine and is yours to use and direct, through you but not from you!"

Later that year, just before the start of the holiday season, I had been feeling "down", tired, etc. This reading was given on November 21, 1991.

God: "Things are better, are they not? We are providing. Keep faith with Us and We will stand by you. Your energy is still low and you don't feel 'great', but you will improve. Life will cease to be the chore it is now. You will soon have an influx of vitality. Use it well and do not waste it.

"Why are you concerned about psychic powers and abilities? Realization of oneness is most important but you do have more power than you realize. Continue as you are doing and be not concerned with trivialities. Live each day as best you can and keep the faith.

"It was all right to miss going to level when you felt so exhausted. We are not tyrants. It is for your own good to do this as well as helping others. We are pleased with you and soon you will see more proof of this in your inner and outer life. Be not impatient. All goes as planned!"

# DREAMS

I will dwell very briefly on dreams and their importance in helping us to solve problems. They explain events and tell us what is going on in different levels of our lives.

We should all keep dream journals, writing down all we remember as soon as we awaken. If we have a vivid and powerful dream and awaken after it during the night, it is best to write it down then. If we don't, we may forget important details. Also, as soon as possible, we should meditate on the meaning or meanings of it and relate it to our lives and problems. It may be possible to have someone else interpret it, but they must understand our symbols and what they mean to us.

For instance, if there is a dog in your dream, how do you feel about dogs? Do you like them, dislike them? Are you afraid of them? The dog will symbolize someone or something in your life so all this can make a difference. What was the dog doing and how did you feel about it? Many aspects can enter into a correct interpretation.

I do recommend a good book of your own choice on dreams. It would be of help. I prefer a spiritually oriented one, as that type would be more helpful to me. However, since spiritual growth is an individual process, we must all choose our own way.

I am including a few dreams I've had at different times and my interpretation of them.

I dreamed I was in an alabaster palace. I was poorly dressed in a brown, knee-length gown. Suddenly, a huge tiger was chasing me. I ran down long hallways, up and down steps and finally down a long, winding stairway into a basement. It was the place in the palace where butchers slaughtered animals for the kitchen. There were long tables with a gutter to wash the blood and entrails into a sewer. There was a strong, steady flow of water to keep the gutter clean. I seized one of the huge cleavers that was hanging on the wall behind me. I swung the cleaver at the tiger and killed it as it leaped at me. Then I went back up the stairs to the very top floor and came into a spacious room. In the center of the room was a large tent of soft, transparent material. Seated in the center of the tent was a woman dressed in rich garments. I knew her to be the queen and my mother. She was fondly tending to two small children, a boy and a girl. She would pay no attention to me. She was angry with me because I didn't comply with her concept of a "proper" child. She loved the two little ones because they obeyed her and didn't question her.

In each corner of the tent, facing into the corners sat women, four in all. They were very solemn and ignored everyone, including each other, and sat staring into the corners.

Finally, the king came into the room. He was very angry with the queen, my mother, for her neglect of me. He said to her, "This is my daughter, a princess, and you will treat her as such from now on!"

Next, I was richly dressed and had become a young woman. I was walking with my father, the king, through the castle.

We came into a room where a handsome young man was lying on a white marble platform. He was dead and had been prepared for a funeral. I felt very sad because I loved him. He was my brother and had been in line to be the next king.

My father then took me into another room with one long wall open to the outside. Since we were up very high, I could see for a great distance. My father said I was now his heir and that all I could see would be mine.

Interpretation given at level...

In the first part of the dream, the palace represents my body. The tiger represents various illnesses that were life threatening. The many rooms and stairwells he chased me in were different parts of my body. Had he caught me in any one of them, I could have died.

The basement where food was processed represented my body's digestive system and here I finally faced the tiger and killed it.

The water flowing through and cleansing the gutter indicated how essential it is for me to drink a lot of water to cleanse my system constantly.

The deeper meaning of this part of the dream is that the tiger represents the baser instincts of my nature...they pursue me until going deep within myself (the basement). I face them and overcome them. In this interpretation, the water represents the cleansing of our souls by the Christ within.

In the second part of the dream, the queen mother depicts the church I was brought up in. When I started to ask questions and not accept everything I was told, I became an outcast and was left to fend for myself.

(This didn't actually happen in my life, but it indicates the attitude of so many religions when people want and need to find their own answers.)

The ladies in the corners were other churches-other religions who were isolated by their own choice. They had nothing to do with anyone else and could see nothing else because they only looked in their corner.

The king, of course, is God, my Father, who is displeased with the attitude of the church and insists that I be treated with respect even though I didn't accept all that was told to me.

The dead prince represents the male-oriented bible and views of my former church and others. These viewpoints must "die" and women be given their proper place.

I felt sorrow for this in my dream because I was raised with my brother and loved him.


Another dream....

I dreamed I was watching a huge pupa of a butterfly. As I watched it, a very large yellow butterfly emerged. I thought this meant the dream was for a dear friend of mine, as yellow butterflies are symbols of good luck for her. As soon as I thought this, the butterfly immediately changed into a huge multicolored butterfly signifying it was meant for me. It picked me up by my hair with claws resembling an eagle's talons. It carried me to the top of a mountain. (This didn't hurt me.) As I stood on the mountaintop, I noticed a mound in front of me with what appeared to be the top part of a large glass ball protruding from it. As I looked at it, it rose up and I saw it was actually a large eye. It came forward and went into my forehead.

Given at inner level...

My interpretation of this dream is as follows:

In the beginning of the life of this body, the entity was tightly bound up by the restricting moves and inhibitions of a strict father and a religious environment that gave little leeway to freedom of thought and expression. (Represented by the pupa.) As the body and mind developed, more time than ordinarily given by young people was taken to think deeply about many things. This resulted in opening the mind to thinking metaphysically. (The lifting to the mountain top.)

After learning to meditate and go within to altered states of consciousness, the gift of the "all-seeing eye" was given. This resulted in the many psychic and spiritual gifts being bestowed on the mind and future indwelling personalities.

As dreams often have more than one meaning, this may well be only one interpretation of several, but this is the one that I felt related very concisely with "my" life in the time that the dream occurred.


Dream of Number One...

I dreamed of a snake that threatened to kill me by coiling around me, but someone came along to help me and I was able to stretch it out and kill it.

Interpretation...

The snake that was coiled around me, squeezing the life out of me represented my first marriage. In my dream, I stretched it out so I could kill it. (I had stayed married for almost 40 years!) When I left I felt I had done all I could and felt free to leave.

Another time, I dreamed I had purchased a house from an older woman. I saw a picture practically embedded in the wall over a fireplace. I felt that if I moved it, I would find a hidden wall safe, which I did. It was as large as the picture and had several coats of paint over it. It could barely be seen except that I noticed a crack along the edge and a keyhole. I managed to open it. The former owner appeared and peevishly said that the contents of the safe were hers. I told her that I intended for her to have them. I removed the contents and gave them to her-gold plated candlesticks and various sized (all small) carved objects, mostly human figurines.

Interpretation...

This dream represents my being a walk-in. The house represents the body I took over from the former resident who feels she is the sole owner of the contents of the safe- (the mind and memories) of the house (body) she lived in. I gave them to her willingly (because the body and brain always retain the memories) but as a walk-in, I was also entitled to them. I felt cheated in the dream because these items were supposed to be part of the purchase.

So I went back to sleep and in a continuation of the dream, I saw her willingly return the treasures as she didn't need them anymore and I did!

In still another dream I was trying to jump high, but every time I tried, a small child I had been caring for (not mine) clutched me and kept me from jumping into the air.

Finally, I explained to her that if she let me jump high by myself, I'd pick her up after that and jump with her.

Interpretation...

This dream was telling me that I needed to be alone so I could achieve heights on the inner plane that I was capable of attaining. Then, I could more readily be able to help others.

In the following dream, I was in a building used for meetings, classes, etc. I had gone into a restroom to touch up my hair, makeup, etc. I came out and was saying good-bye to two people, an older man and woman. They seemed to be more elegant than the rest of the people. I went out of my way to impress upon them how much I enjoyed meeting them, especially the woman. (I had given her my right hand and my left hand to the man.)

After they left, I went back into the restroom and looked into the mirror. I realized I hadn't finished fixing my hair. It was sticking up on top, so I looked for my purse to get my comb from it. It wasn't on the counter where I had left it. Then I thought that perhaps I was in the wrong restroom. I went out into the hall and started looking into several restrooms, but couldn't find my purse.

In the meantime, there was a very small girl, toddler size, who was looking for her mother and calling out to her in the hallway. (The little girl had a mature face and spoke very well. She was slender and had an olive complexion.) Her mother came into view, crossing the hall. The little girl, although relieved to find her, called out; "I hate you!" However, the mother seemed unconcerned.

I finally found my purse and was in a car, going home. I decided to see if anything was missing from my purse. I discovered my money was gone as well as my wallet with my driver's license, credit cards, and my makeup kits. I opened my purse wide, held my hands over it, and visualized all my things back in it as well as any merchandise gotten with my credit cards to be back in the stores as if it had not been purchased. Thus, it would be as if no one had taken my purse or anything from it.

In my dream, I did not feel as relaxed as I should have been after this. In fact, I was quite angry and awakened at this point without knowing if my things had really been returned.

Interpretation...

The elegant man and woman represented Mother/Father God. I wanted to make very sure that they understood what an honor it was to meet them.

Giving the woman my right hand indicated that she was the dominant God-aspect in my life in this lifetime.

Losing my purse in which my valuables were kept could mean I was concerned over the possibility of losing my psychic gifts. (Perhaps I didn't feel as capable as I had been.) The purse could also represent the mind of the former occupant of my body. She had been very active metaphysically. Realizing that my valuables were not in the purse could express disappointment at what I felt was a lack in my psychic abilities. I tried to bring back my "missing" things by using my hands to heal the situation. I awoke angry because I felt unsure of the outcome.

Throughout my active metaphysical life, there have been times that I have felt inadequate. I have often felt I should do more, do better. At these times, I'd be given reading to explain these apparent "dry spells". I include some of these in the section titled Readings.

The part of the previous dream concerning the little girl could reflect my search for enlightenment and higher spirituality. I couldn't find it in "Mother Church", so I felt lost, alienated. The unconcerned mother was a representation of how I felt the church perceived me.

It is interesting to me that the little girl was small but mature in her face and speech. I was very small all during my growing years. Also, she was dark complected as I was until later in life. (My olive skin became very fair, my brown eyes developed a blue rim, and I became a blonde.)

Also, even growing up in a family of five children I always felt rather apart and alone...lost, like the little girl in the dream. No matter now involved I became in group activities, at the same time, I always felt like an outsider, not quite one with the group- again depicted in the dream by the little girl, alone and lost in a crowd of people. But I never felt lonely!

This dream demonstrates how one dream can touch on many subjects and different times.

The following dream seemed very simple, but had many deep meanings which I will try to make as simple as possible because the more I got into the interpretation, the more confusing it seemed.

Dream...

I was trying to use a mirror that was mounted on a pedestal. The mirror part was very wobbly. I tried to tighten it by turning a plate on the bottom of the pedestal. There were instructions imprinted in the plate that this was the proper procedure to follow. Doing this, however, failed to correct the wobble. Finally, I decided to turn the plate in the opposite direction and the mirror became strong, steady, stable. This was a very old mirror-an antique. The stand represented my mind-the mirror is that part through which I see myself. To make my mind what it should be, I had to turn my thinking around. In other words, the old instructions no longer worked. What might have seemed true at one time was no longer valid.

# MEDITATION

I have put this chapter last, but it is most important. Without meditation, much of what I discuss in this book may not have happened. It opened the door to the spiritual world for me and changed my life in so many beneficial ways.

In writing of meditation, I use ideas from many teachers and include thoughts and experiences of my own.

Meditation is the key to realization of union with God, which is the reason for our existence on the earth. Without meditation, it is impossible to achieve true realization of union and the accompanying spiritual evolution.

While it is true that many people have experienced the benefits of meditation without using or even knowing a definite method for doing so, it is necessary to achieve the proper state of consciousness to truly experience union with the True Self.

Many enlightened souls have entered into a contemplative or daydream state regularly, while concentrating on a spiritual concept or in a worshipful state of mind and have experienced the desired result, but it is usually helpful to have a definite method for entering into the proper state of awareness. All teachers of meditation are in agreement that relaxation of mind and body is the first step and contemplation next.

After one becomes accustomed to the state of mind that brings on a meditative condition, it is possible to achieve this state at will and anywhere. But until this is possible, it is best to practice under ideal conditions as described here:

In order to become relaxed, it is best to feel as comfortable as possible. It is recommended that the clothing be loose, the temperature comfortable, and the light dim. (As one becomes accustomed to meditating, these conditions may not be so important, but they are the ideal conditions.) One may lie down or sit up, as long as the spine is kept straight. It is often suggested that burning incense with an agreeable scent and having soft music playing is conducive to relaxation and to inducing the right atmosphere-it is an individual thing. I personally prefer it to be quiet.

All meditation techniques are similar in that all involve a focusing of attention. It is thought that concentrating on a candle flame, a blank wall, a crystal, one's own breathing, or a certain sound or other such things may be helpful. I found that I preferred not using any of these aids since I didn't want to be dependent on them and they might not be available everywhere. But again, it is a personal choice.

Concentration causes the awareness to narrow to a fine point and break through to a higher plane. Meditation has been found to increase the alpha brainwave production in the frontal and central regions of the brain, whereas the normal alpha cycle is generally found in the occipital area at the back of the head.

Those who practice meditation have been found to be happier, more relaxed, to have developed deeper personal relationships, and to have more personal resources. Empathy and openness seem to increase as well. It also has a calming influence and the heart rate slows down; creativity and intuition are increased.

The physical benefits derived from the meditative state are being increasingly acknowledged by the medical profession, especially since these benefits can now be scientifically measured by the use of various types of biofeedback machines. These machines show indisputable proof that altered states of consciousness can actually bring about measurable changes of activity in various parts of the body.

In any metaphysical book, there is almost certain to be at least a reference to meditation and/or altered states of consciousness, as all writers with any degree of knowledge on even a related subject recognize the importance of the meditative state in achieving contact with the Inner Power or Self and the benefits and abilities to be derived from this practice.

Swami Muktananda states that the true purpose of meditation is connection with the inner self, or God, and this is the goal of life. He teaches that meditation is easy, natural and spontaneous; it merely shifts the focus of our attention from the outside to the inside. It is not an activity that one performs, but a state that one "slips" into, like falling asleep.

The Swami says there are many techniques which are supposed to lead us to God, but of all these, meditation is the one recognized by saints and sages because only in meditation do we go within ourselves to that place where the inner Self dwells. Logical reasoning cannot achieve this union either. When the Self is within, he asks, why do we look for knowledge of it elsewhere? Through meditation, he says, we can be healed. It improves our abilities to do various things; we travel to different inner planes and have many different experiences. In addition, he writes that meditation brings inner happiness and peace that it is fine to have visions, but they are not necessary. What is necessary is inner joy-"When all the senses become quiet and you experience bliss, that is the attainment." He is, of course, referring here to union with the True Self. He quotes the Upanishads as teaching that we cannot attain the True Self by doing good actions or by performing rituals, but only through our own direct knowledge of God which comes only through meditation.

Emily Cady tells us that everyone must take time daily for quiet and meditation as no one can grow in either spiritual knowledge or power without it. She says it is as necessary to practice the presence of God as one would practice music if one would excel in that subject, that meditating daily alone with God serves to focus the Divine Presence within one and bring it to our consciousness. The attitude should be that of waiting upon God and listening for God's voice. She tells us that meditation is the only way that one gains definite knowledge, true wisdom, newness of experience, steadiness of purpose, and power to meet the unknown.

Dr. M.M. Bhamgara compares our True Self to the bottom of the ocean, serene and tranquil no matter what may be occurring on the surface. This True Self may be reached, he says, by relaxing and "learning to enter the quiet room within." Thus, we build a foundation for sound mental health and so become truly "untouchable" instead of "touchy". He states that from a purely mental hygiene point of view, we require "mental fasting", or meditation, and he recommends relaxation not only for sound mental health, but also as helping on all planes of our triumvirate being.

William James quotes Dr. R. M. Bucks as saying cosmic consciousness is not simply an expansion or extension of the familiar self-conscious mind, but actually an addition of a function distinctly different from any possessed by the average person. Along with cosmic consciousness, there occurs an intellectual enlightenment, which alone would make the person experiencing it almost a member of a new species. He adds that there is a state of exaltation, a feeling that one will not only have eternal life, but already has it. He is describing, of course, the feeling of experiencing union with the inner and True Self with which students of metaphysics are familiar.

William James himself says that in India, training in mystical insight has been known since time immemorial under the name of Yoga, which means union with the Divine. It is, he says, based on persevering in various exercises, diet, posture, breathing, intellectual concentration, and moral discipline through which the practitioner eventually may enter into the condition called "Samudhi" and comes face to face with facts which no instinct or reason can ever know. The mind itself, he writes, has a higher state beyond reason and when this state is reached the truth shines forth and we know ourselves.

According to Vedantists, James says, if one stumbles into super-consciousness sporadically (as opposed to experiencing it as a result of regular practice) he or she is then "impure" or subject to loss of it. This premise appears to give credit to the practice of Yoga rather than to meditation alone for finding God within, saying in effect, that one must combine all the aforementioned practices in order for the discovery of the True Self within to be authentic.

This is not necessarily James' own viewpoint (nor is it mine); he is merely presenting the beliefs of the Vedantists. Down through the ages, many have found God within who meditated only. I find no fault with those who practice Yoga-each of us must choose our own path to enlightenment.

Using meditation to improve your life is the main theme in Earnest Holmes' book, "Science of Mind". He states that one who wishes to work out his problems must take the time to meditate daily and treat the condition mentally. He gives no methods for meditating per say, but does give many suggestions as to how to think about problems and treat them, as well as explaining God's nature and attributes in accordance with metaphysical thinking. Mr. Holmes says that the mind that we discover within us is the mind, which governs everything, and we should recognize the simplicity of this fact. He describes his book as not a special revelation of any individual, but rather the culmination of all revelations.

In describing the soul's striving to attain the divine state by it's own efforts, Alan Watts says it falls into total despair until suddenly "there dawns upon it with a great illuminative shock the realization that the divine state simply is here and now and does not have to be attained." Here he is telling us, as do all metaphysical teachers, that God is already within us, that we need only to seek within ourselves. Later, he reiterates that almost all mysticism, Western or Eastern, has the sense of "given-ness" of union which has only to be recognized and accepted, not achieved.

According to Dr. Herbert Benson, meditation may be the best "medicine" of all because a healing hormone is produced when the mind is relaxed. He says practicing meditation for ten to twenty minutes twice a day leads to a permanent protective mechanism in the body. This mechanism is activated by a hormone called norepinephrine, which is produced by the brain in large quantities when a person meditates. The healing effect of this hormone, he tells us, can eliminate migraine headaches and high blood pressure. It can slow body metabolism and calm an over stressed heart. He goes on to say it also results in mental calmness because of the mind's and body's response to this hormone's effects. This is the same hormone produced by the body in moments of psychological or physical stress and protects a person's reflexes in emergencies-the fight or flight syndrome. When a body is relaxed, however, the hormone acts as a healing and soothing agent. According to the article, there are several drugs being used to treat high blood pressure which react in the same way, but those using relaxation techniques (as in meditation) will experience a sense of well-being in addition to physical benefits. So here again, we find that the scientist is in agreement with the metaphysician who has known these things to be true for ages.

It is interesting to observe that all the authors included in this chapter, as well as those in most books on meditation and related subjects state their beliefs in very positive phrases. Nowhere does one observe the authors using such phrases as ""I think this is true, or I feel this is possible", etc. On the contrary, their statements are ones of fact and truth with no ambivalence whatever. This positive attitude is the result of the inner confidence and knowledge of truth acquired from practicing some form of meditation regularly.

The advantage of learning to meditate without having to assume a certain posture, ritual, or use an aid of any kind is obvious since one can then "go within" at any time or in any place and experience the many benefits of meditation when they may be needed.

Serious students of meditation are in accord that in meditation we use God's greatest gift to humanity-our mind. It is the means of our evolution as well as a tool to make our lives what we want them to be. In mind we are truly one with the Divine Mind. Our awareness and realization of this while in a meditative state removes all feelings of separation and thus we experience our true state of being.

Teachers of meditation invariably state that as one becomes accustomed to meditating, it is necessary to keep an open mind and be willing to give up all former beliefs because as we evolve spiritually, our understanding increases and many things we have previously accepted as truth are now revealed as illusion. We are also made aware of many truths that we have never consciously thought about.

Teachers also usually inform students that increased psychic awareness and abilities may also be a result of practicing meditation, but these things should not be the goal of any seeker of truth. Becoming too intrigued by these abilities could be a real obstruction to spiritual growth in that they may become the focal point of our concentration instead of God realization.

As a result of meditation, the various psychic centers are opened or activated. This is caused, as we have seen, by the rising of the vibratory pattern of the meditation. It causes access to the inner on higher levels, which correspond to that peculiar vibration. This, in turn, can result in contact with the entities on each plane or level as we progress.

It has been my observation that entities from higher planes can descend to lower planes, but those on the lower planes cannot ascend higher until their vibratory level is equal to those on the next plane. An exception to this may occur if an entity from a lower level is escorted by one or more beings from a higher level.

Also, I have observed entities on various levels simultaneously, but each on their own plane and in proper order. It was explained to me that entities on each plane or level are concerned primarily with the duties inherent to that plane. For instance, those on the mental plane are interested in and involved with increasing the awareness and expanding the minds of humanity. Those on the spiritual level are involved with improving and increasing the spirituality of humans, but they cooperate with entities on all levels for the benefit of mankind. Each entity that is on one level is raising it's own vibrations so that it might enter the next higher level.

The only way we can achieve an increase and raising of our vibrations, and it is vitally important for spiritual growth to do so daily, is meditation. The more often and more deeply one meditates, the faster spiritual growth occurs, and the more inner planes one has access to, as well as the more psychic experiences one is apt to have on these planes.

In addition to spiritual enhancement, there are many other advantages to be derived from the meditative state. It has already been shown that one derives an increase in intellectual ability, peace of mind, improved health, and so on, but, in addition to all of these, one can actually change one's life and solve problems on the material plane. There are many techniques taught to achieve this. One is by making positive affirmations while in a light meditative state. This sends out positive vibrations, which attract to us that which we desire. An even more effective method is visualization while in a state of meditation in which one sees the desired goal happily accomplished.

In using either of these techniques, it is important to keep a positive outlook on the conscious level as negative thinking can delay or even negate the desired result. In visualizing a desired result, we use the mind to actually create the condition or result we desire to experience. It is immaterial whether one programs for health, financial or social success, happiness or whatever; it is all the same to Divine Mind. We create it and it becomes a fact.

It is said that prayer is talking to God, and meditation is listening to hear God talking to us. So it is with programming. We actually work with God to bring the good we desire to ourselves and to others.

Spiritual growth is a direct result of meditation, but in order to grow; it is necessary to keep an open mind. As previously stated, new truths will be revealed to us as we grow.

This is in direct opposition to the belief structure of most religions, which teach the necessity of accepting their teachings with blind faith. This actually impedes spiritual growth, because only by questioning and meditating on things about which we wonder or feel doubt can we get to know our own truth and spirituality.

We find, going all the way back in recorded history, all teachers and practitioners of meditation are in agreement as to the many benefits for body, mind and soul that result from meditation regularly, no matter what particular method or technique they may advocate.

Meditation is the only way to realize union with the True Self whether one uses a definite technique to reach a meditative state or it is brought on by a state of reverie.

There have been little, if any changes in meditation techniques since they were first used or developed, except to simplify them. This indicates that it is an inherent ability and need, and no mater what various methods are used, the results are the same. A time set-aside for this upon awakening and before retiring daily will result in a drastic change in an individual that will enhance that person's life in every way.

Since it has been proven by both actual personal experience and scientific study that an individual gains innumerable benefits in so many ways, both tangible and intangible from meditating, it would seem a reasonable conclusion that more use should be made of this marvelous aid to a better life.

I would advocate a form of meditation being taught and practiced in all schools, from the lowest grades and throughout all the levels of education in all countries of the world.

As meditation enhances a person spiritually and brings out the "best" in one, it follows that human nature would be improved, there would be less friction in families, less crime of all kinds and eventually, cessation of wars. Mankind could then use its energies and talents to truly improve conditions for everyone on the planet.

Scientists could make use of the increased awareness of accomplished meditators to get desired information for scientific projects such as new energy sources or better use of the present resources, as well as better ways of doing things in general.

Doctors could make use of these enhanced states to diagnose illnesses and conceive of more effective ways to treat patients. If doctors were themselves meditators they could then project mental healing treatments to their patients as well.

Since only good can come from meditation, it is a logical conclusion that the more people who are involved in practicing it, the more all humanity will benefit from it. This should, indeed, be a goal in the overall education of every human being.

# EPILOGUE

The many things I talk about in this book will never become passé. It is a spiritual journey we must all make eventually, each in our own fashion.

When I finished this book I thought Mega would always be with me. Wrong again! Shortly after I finished the book she left and another oversoul came to me. Her name was Hebecca and she said she came from a higher echelon of angels and she was now my oversoul and guardian angel. For some reason I could never feel as close to her as I did to Mega and I missed Mega very much. However, if I've learned anything from all my experiences it is to not think things will never change but to be open to new experiences. So I accepted Hebecca and felt remiss because I didn't feel the connection I had with her predecessor. Out of curiosity I asked her what she looked like since I never did see her face clearly. She replied - "like you, only perfect"!

'Lo and behold, in a relatively short time I met Hebecca's replacement. She was so beautiful she took my breath away. I asked her what her name was and she replied "Viola". My mother's middle name! I felt close to her immediately. She told me she was from one of the highest echelon of angels. The previous ones were to prepare me for her, again, a necessary raising of my spiritual vibrations.

Since she has been with me some special things have taken place.

First, my daughter had come to help me by doing cleaning for me. She needed a stool to reach something and took a little wooden one from a closet but noticed it was cracked right across the middle. She said, "Mom, this needs to be glued back together". I put it on the floor next to my recliner in the den and didn't think anymore about it. The next night I sat in my recliner and put my hand on the lever to raise the leg rest. It wouldn't work because the little stool was under the handle. I picked it up. Much to my surprise, it was glued together very solidly. I immediately called my daughter and asked her if she had glued it but she said she hadn't. Then I asked my husband if he had glued it had he said, "No, do you want me to?"

Shortly after this on a cool evening I was again sitting in my recliner and decided to use an afghan my mother, who had passed away several years before, had made for me. I seldom used it because it wasn't long enough to cover me from my shoulders to my toes so I had been using a larger one. Imagine my astonishment when I found I could cover my whole body with it and tuck it under my feet. I stood up to see just how long it was now and holding it as tall as it would go it was taller than I. Not only that, but it was also wider. I was flabbergasted and delighted!

Later I asked my new guardian angel if she had fixed the stool. She said no; a little angel she was training did it. (I had noticed it was a little bit crooked!) Then I asked her if she had lengthened and widened the afghan and she said no, my mother had but she, Viola, had made it possible by using her God-given powers to strengthen my Mother's abilities to function on this level.

Other things of a lesser impact have occurred such as my bedroom door closing by itself when I had left it half-open. One day I was feeling irritable. The television was on in the breakfast room. As soon as I came in it turned off. When I walked into the study the television turned on. Later that day the radio turned on by itself and my blood pressure machine would not work for me but it did for my husband.

Of course, we know angels are spirits and have no physical form. They assume one so that we can see and identify them when they come to us on the spiritual level. And, as in some of the true stories I have told about angels in this book, they can also assume very real physical forms. Just recently yet another angel replaced my dear Viola. She was so ethereal she was almost transparent. As the days went on she became more solid and now is totally visible. She had to adjust to this new dimension, as it was so much denser than the one she had come from. She explained to me that she was from the world of "creator angels," the very highest order. She said I might call her Hebe. She also explained to me that each succeeding angel had raised my vibrations so the next could come and now she could be not only my guardian angel but also my soul-the last walk-in?

I told her I felt that she was wasting her vast talents being with me but she said mainly she was adjusting to life on earth so she could be ready to help when the time of tremendous upheaval occurred here. At that time she will become a walk-in to a suitable young body and use her vast God-given powers to help the remaining humans.

I am told that, like me, others on earth are being used to acclimate higher spiritual beings to life on this planet. They will be needed all over the world during and after the great cataclysm. In the meantime they are helping in many ways while in the bodies of their host human beings.

These happenings just serve to prove to me again that there is no end to what we can experience and learn once we start on the path of mental and spiritual evolution.

# About the Author

I was the second of five children and I was the "odd one"-the only brunette, sick a lot, but very athletic in between.

I left school in the junior year of high school due to illness and met my future husband. I knew immediately we would be married and a year-and-a-half later we were.

In my late 40s, raising the last three of my five daughters, I became aware that I was very psychic and a healer. I was deeply into all this when I also became a member of Mensa, got my GED, and took and passed college entrance exams. I planned to become a psychologist as I was deeply into metaphysical counseling by this time and thought it would be helpful. However, on the way to enroll I was told by my "inner guidance" not to do this, "as there is a lot of error in those books." So, I turned around and went home.

At 60, I divorced my first husband, went to a big city where I knew no one and made a new life for myself. I looked very young for my age and had a marvelous time for six years. One day during meditation I was shown a man and told this was my next husband. We met shortly after that and eloped in a few weeks time.

Life continues to be an adventure!